BABIES GALORE

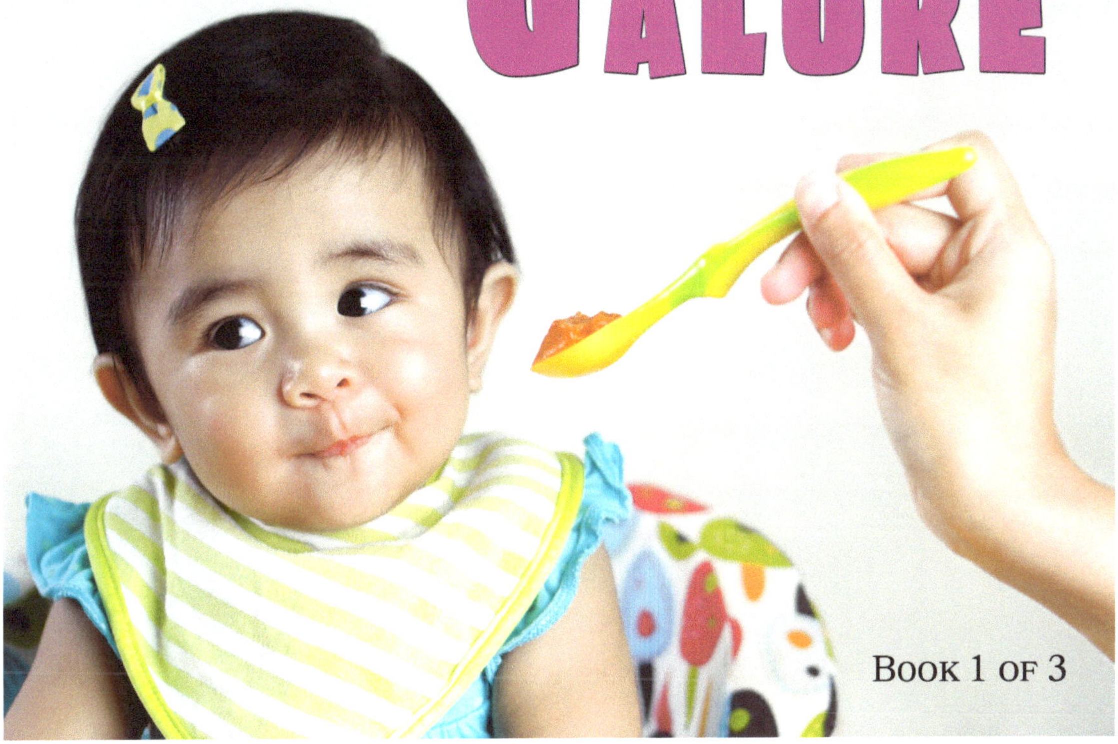

BOOK 1 OF 3

ISBN: 978-1-989842-10-2

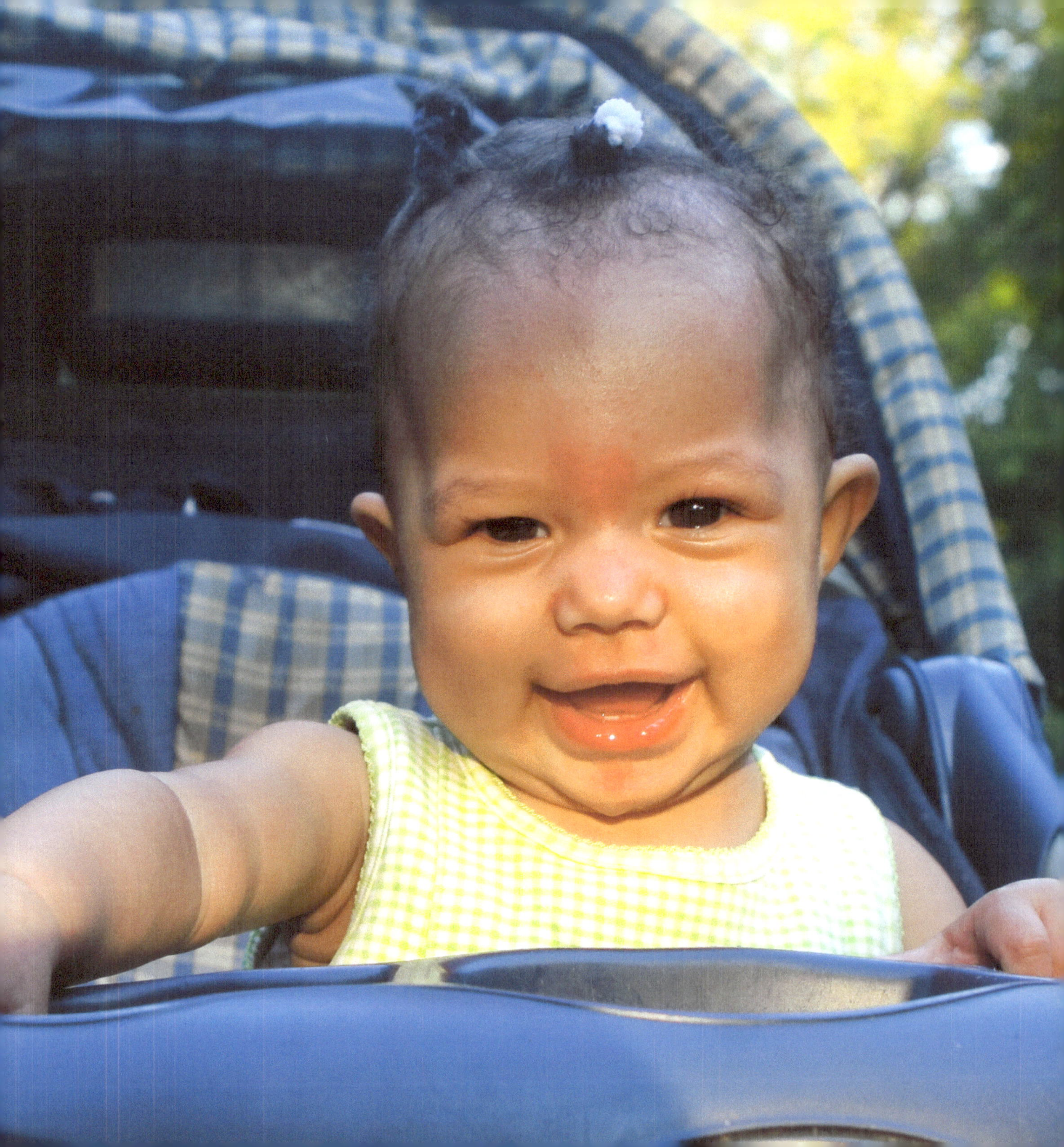

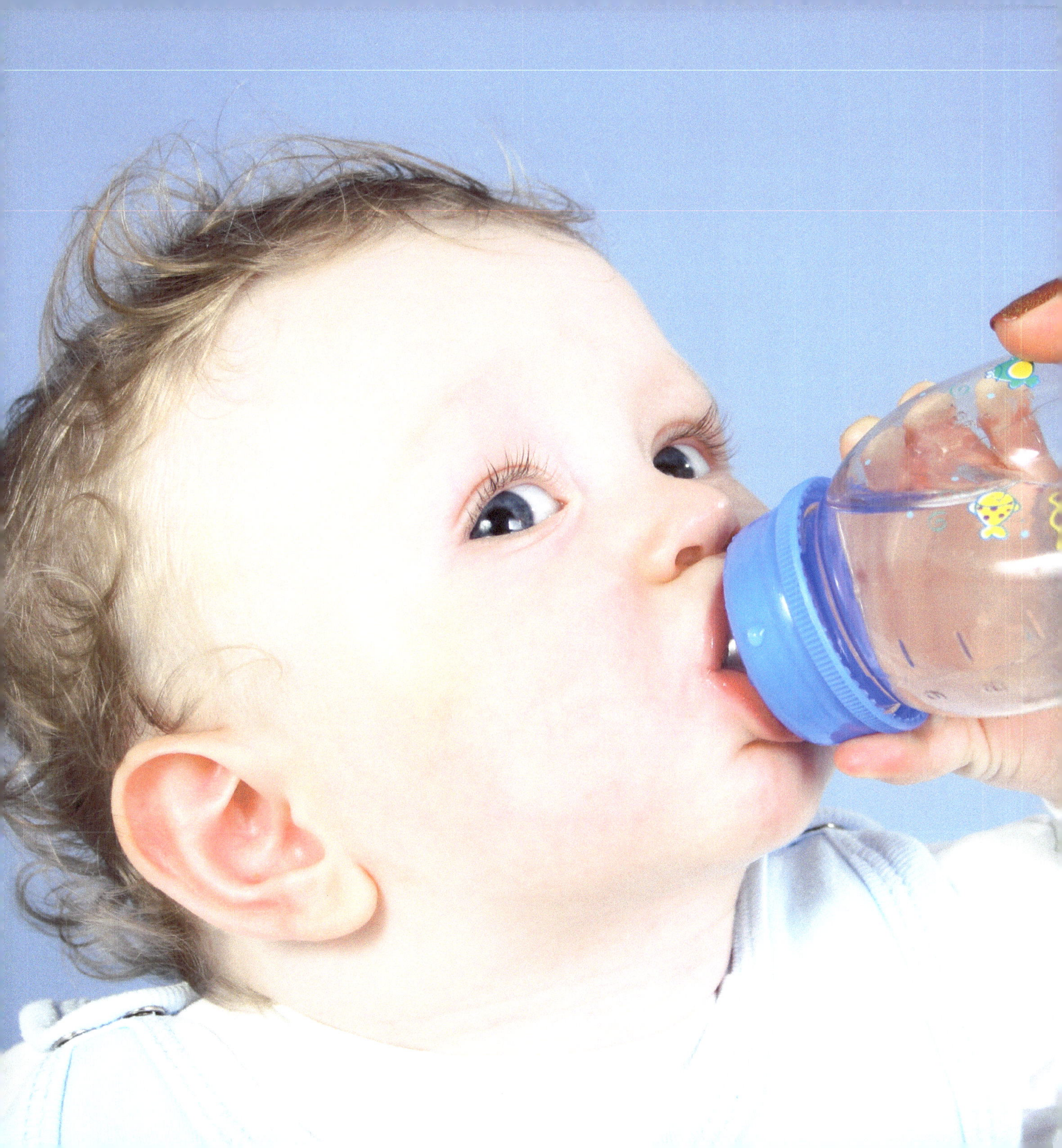

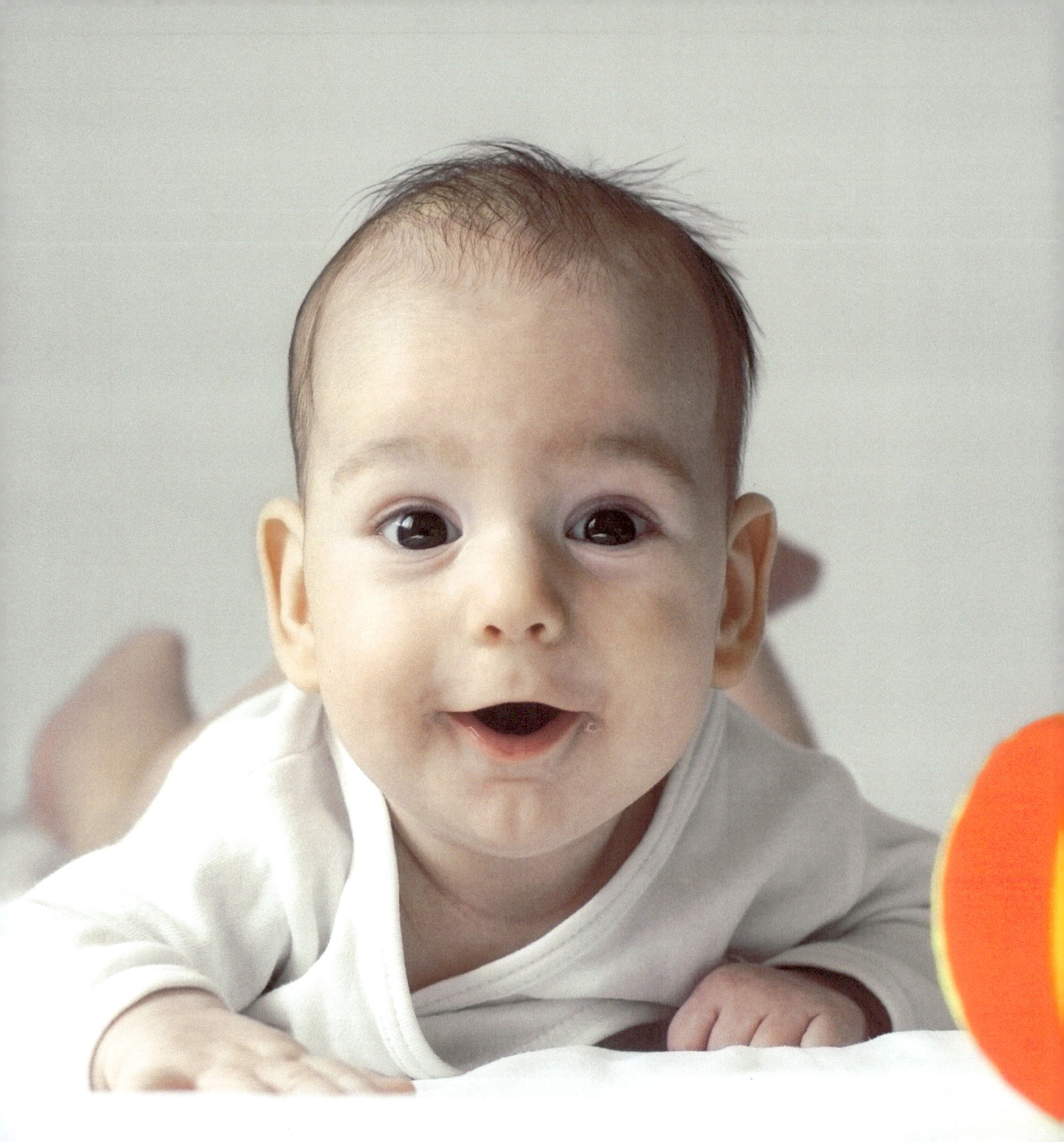

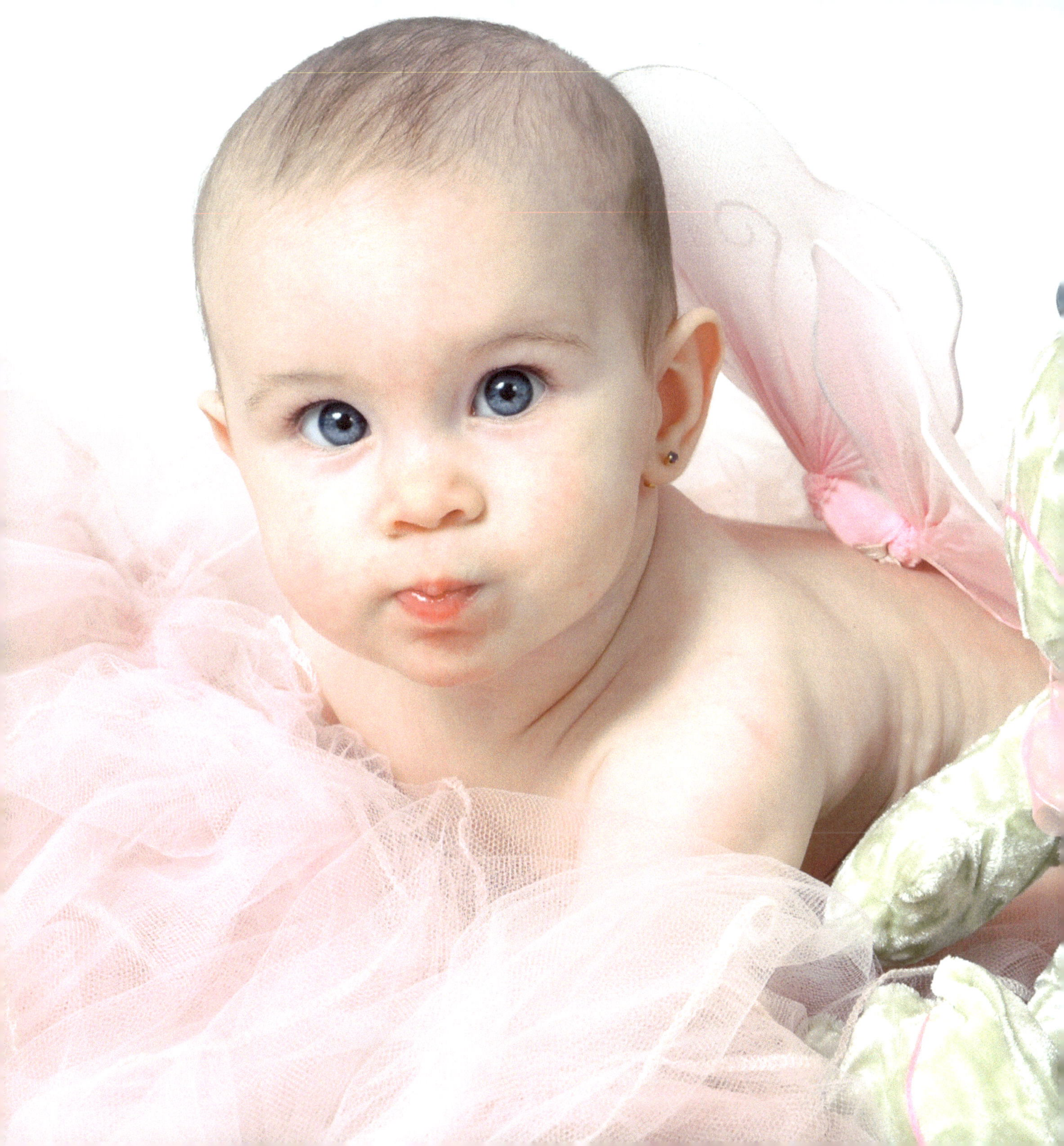

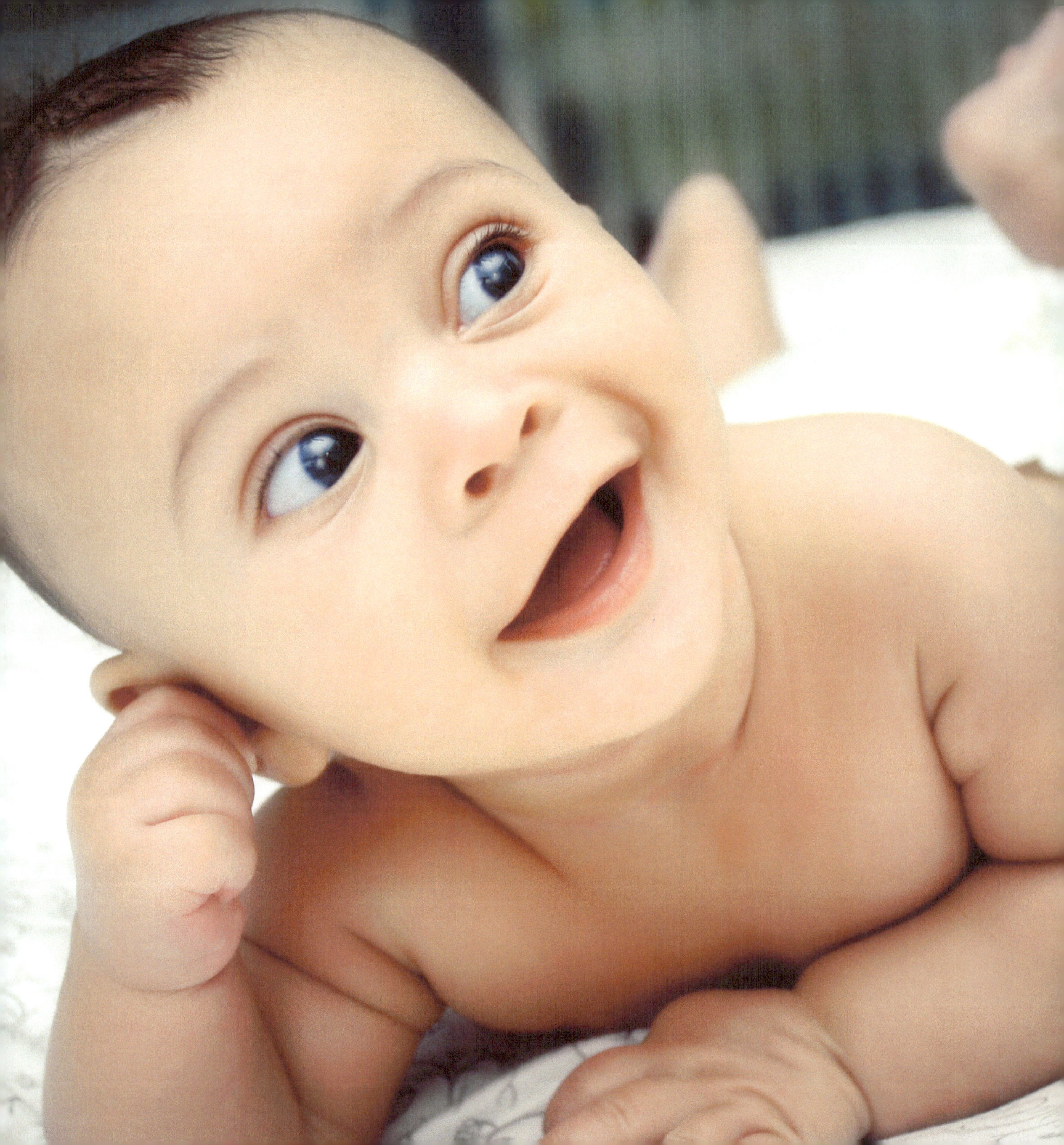

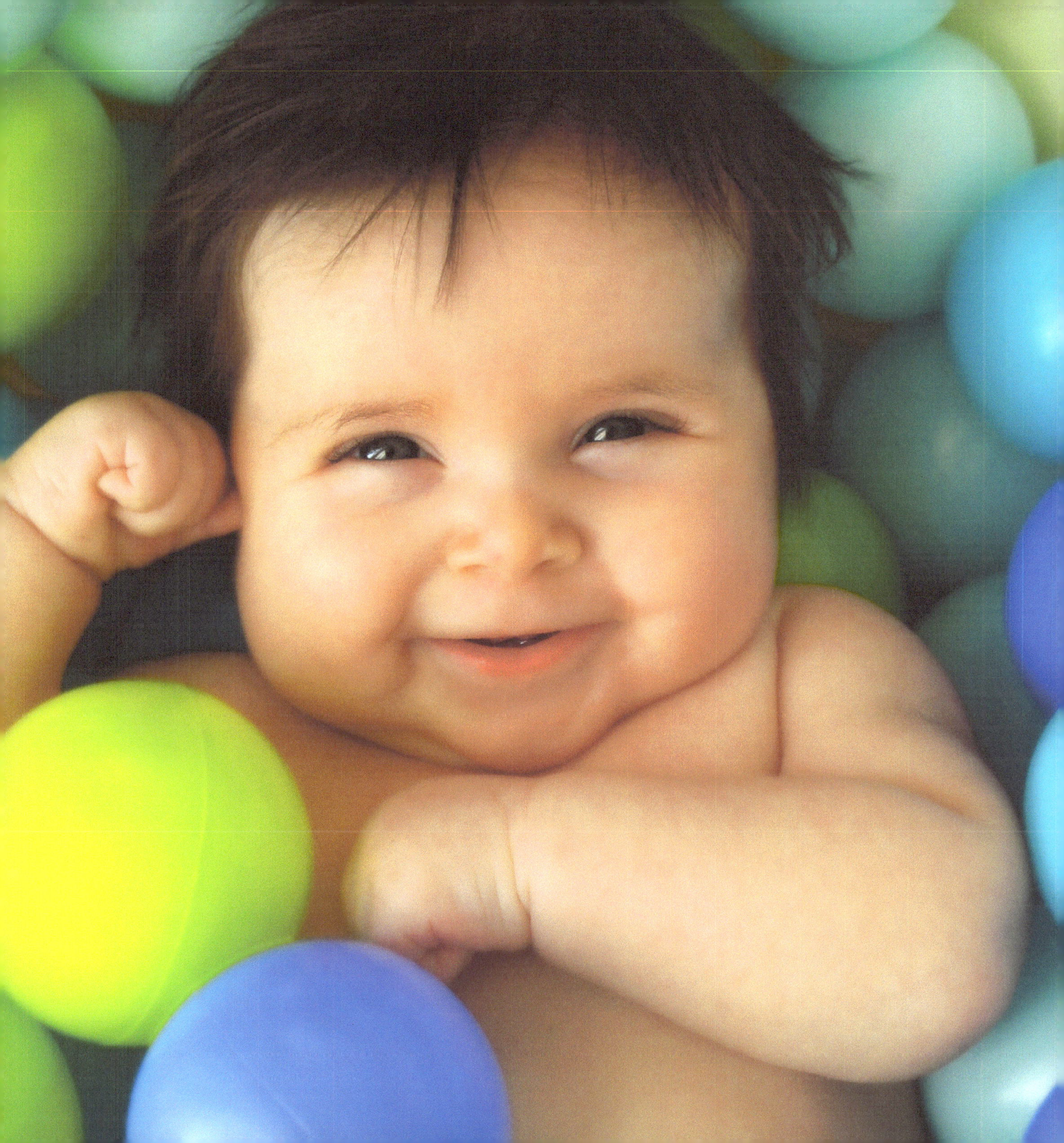

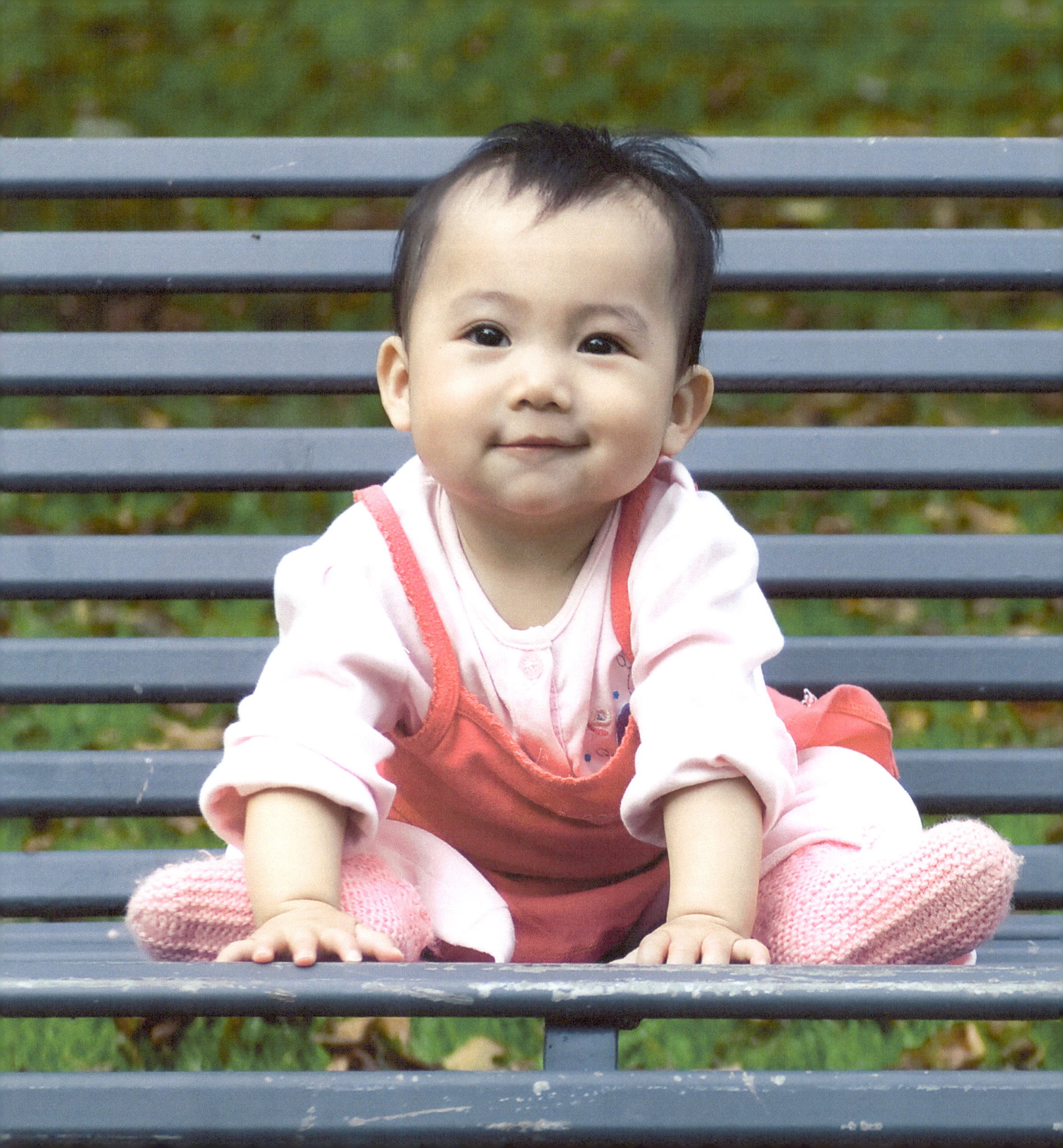

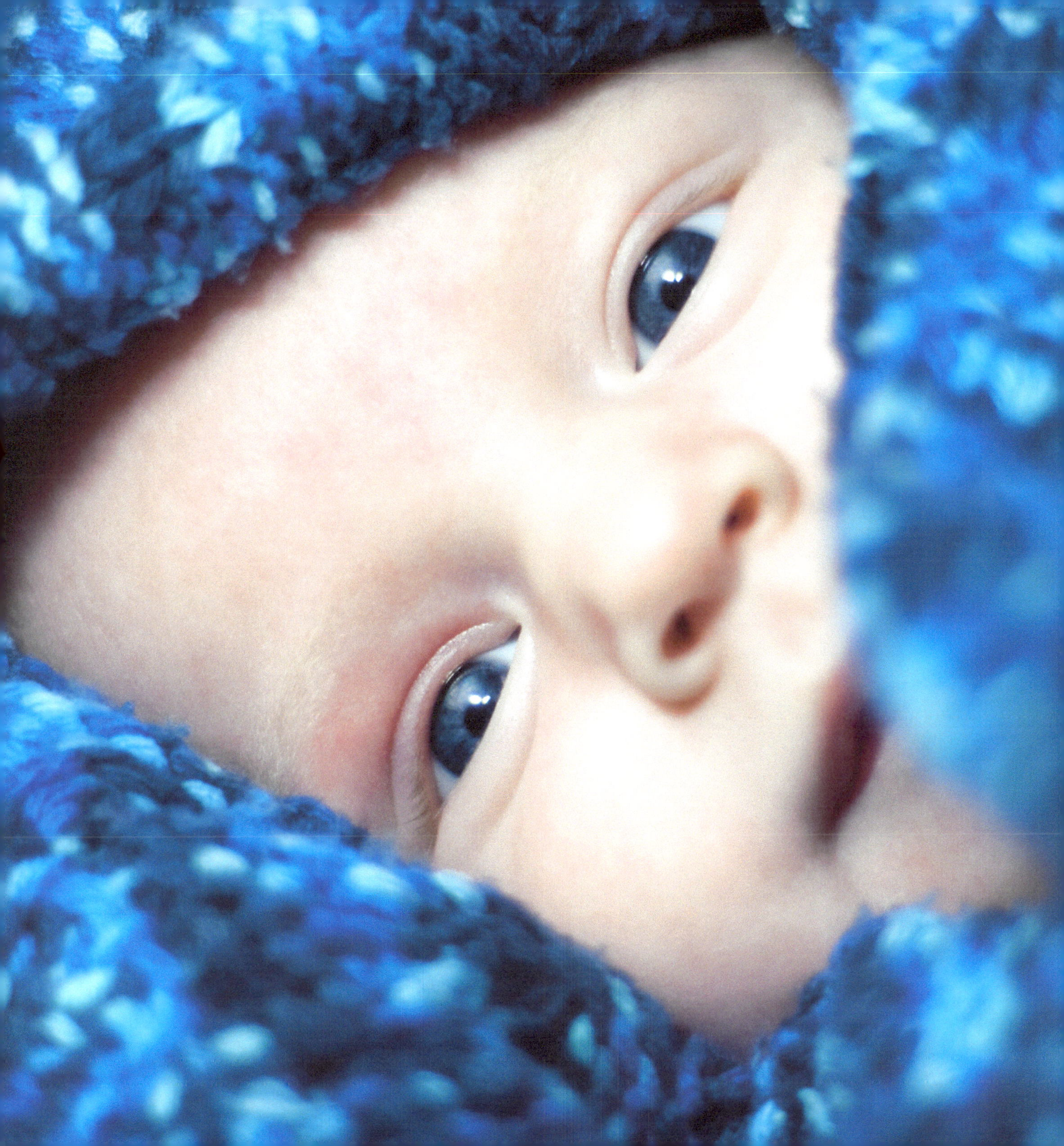

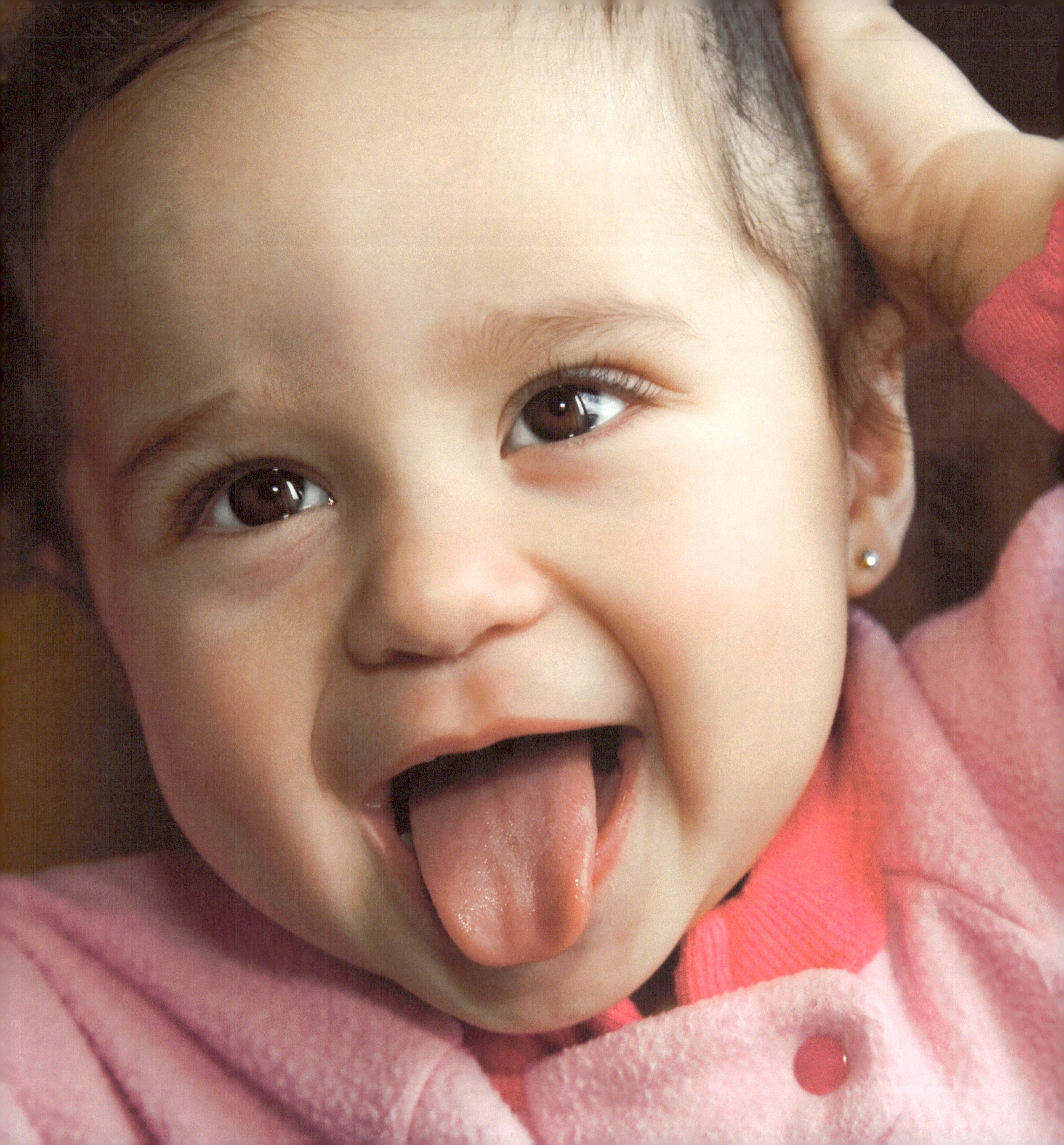

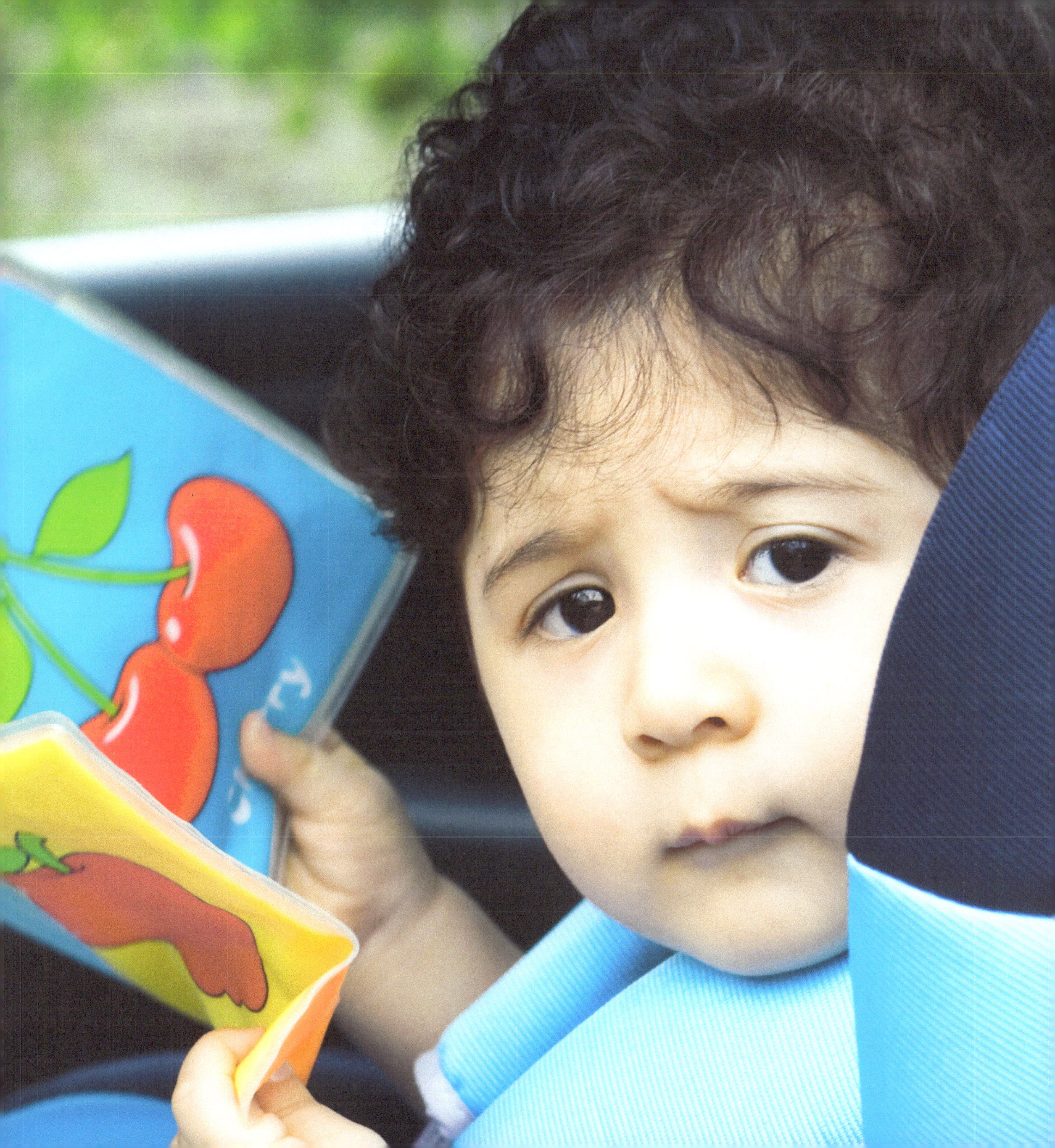

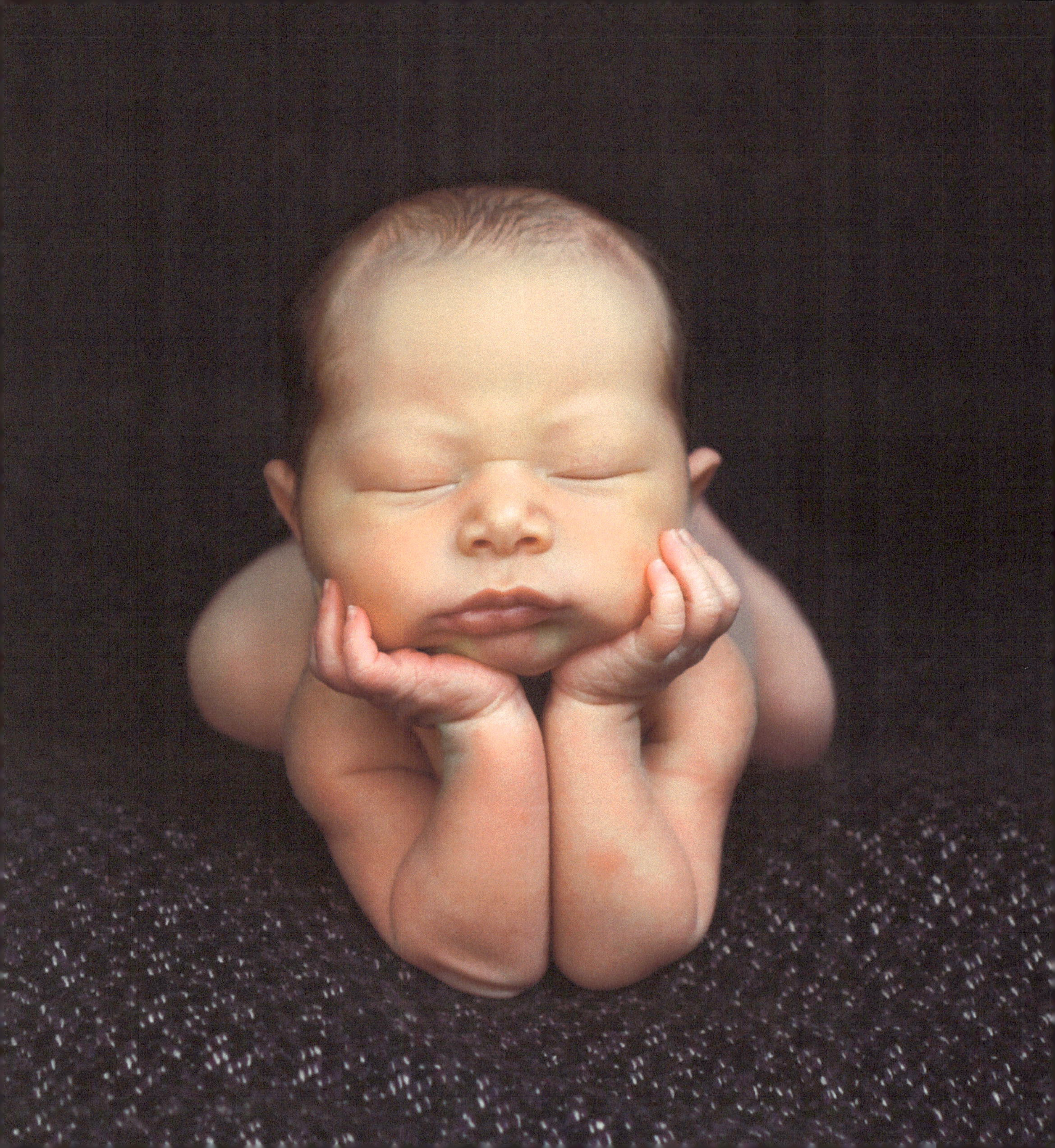

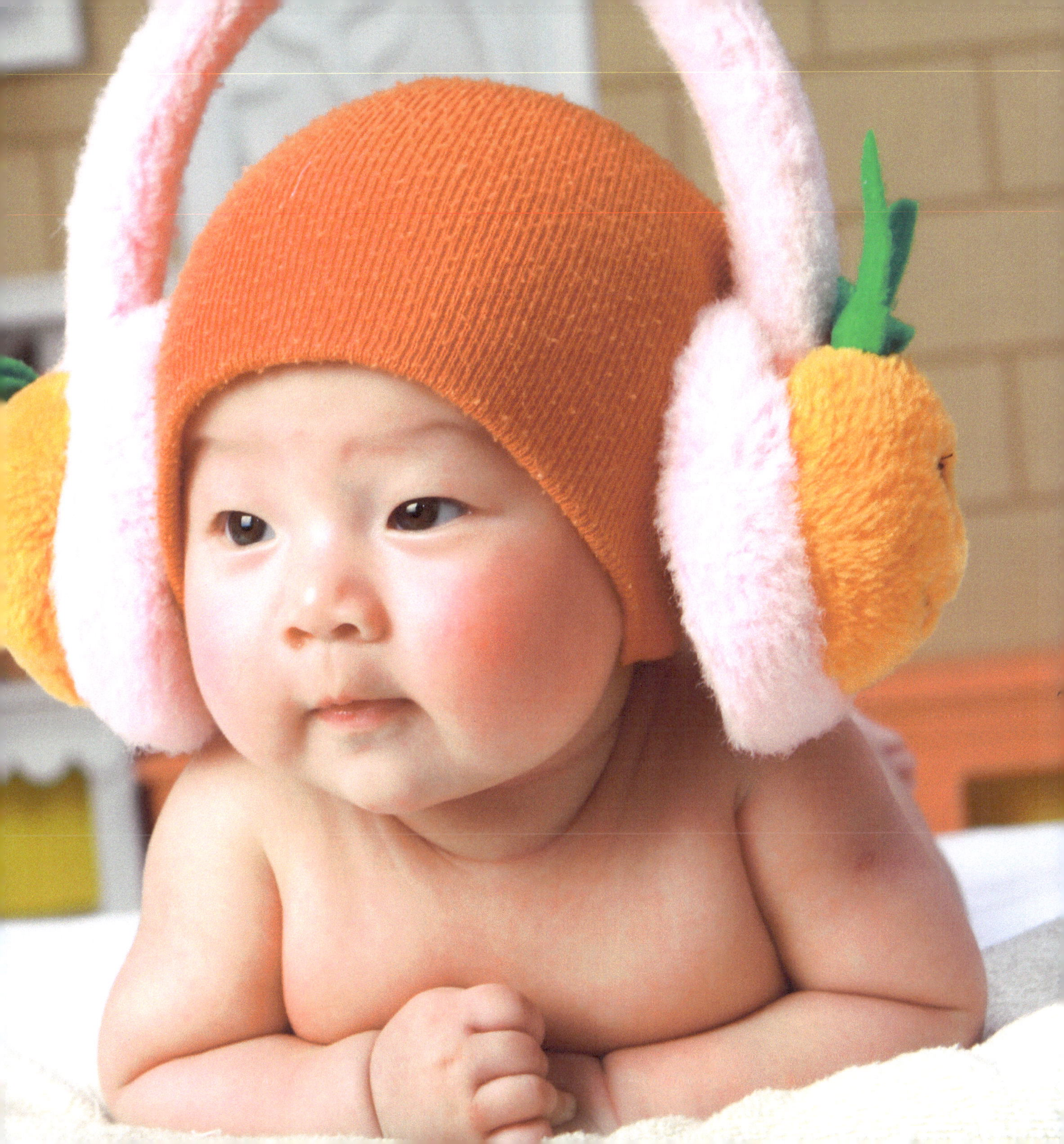

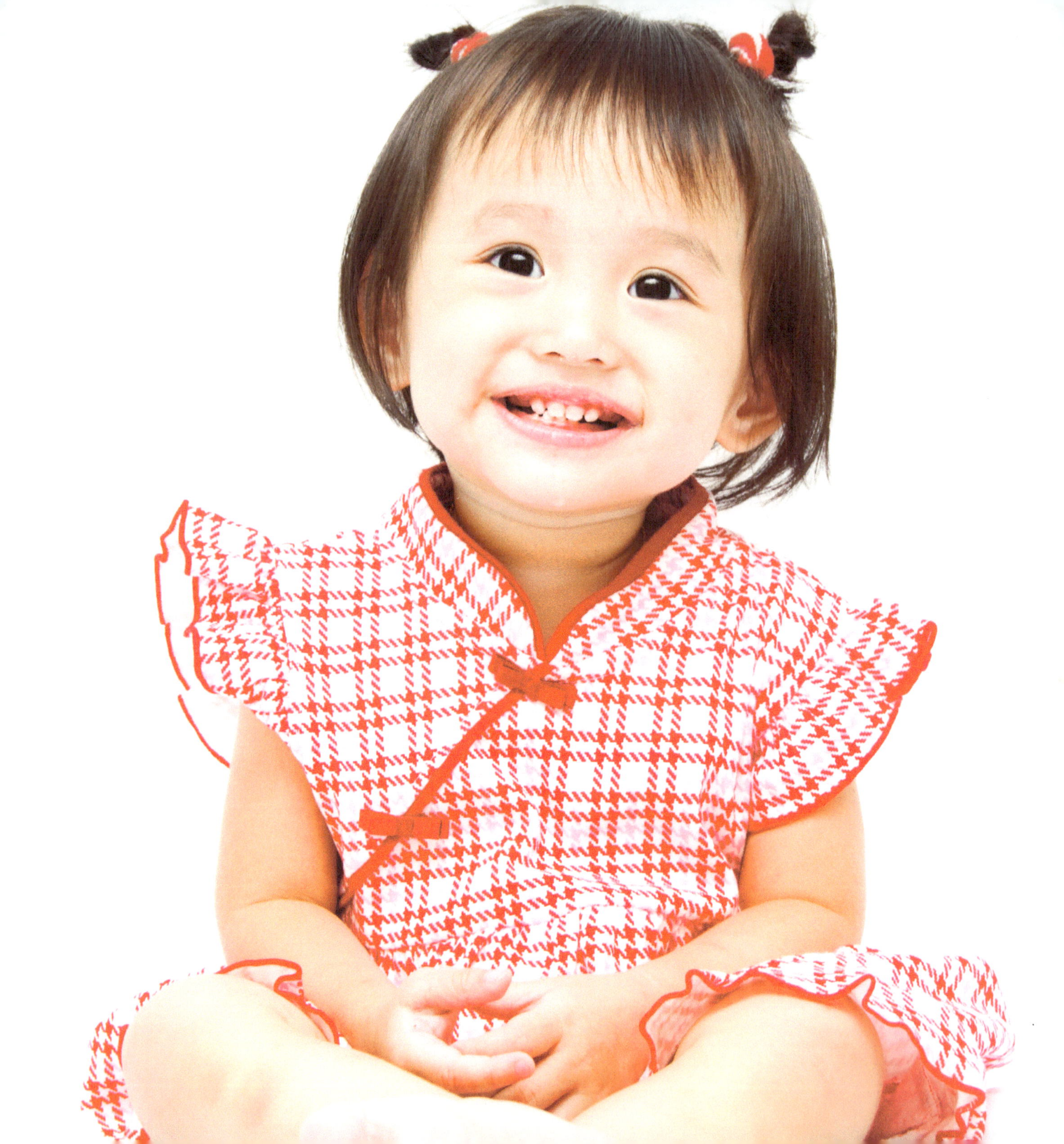

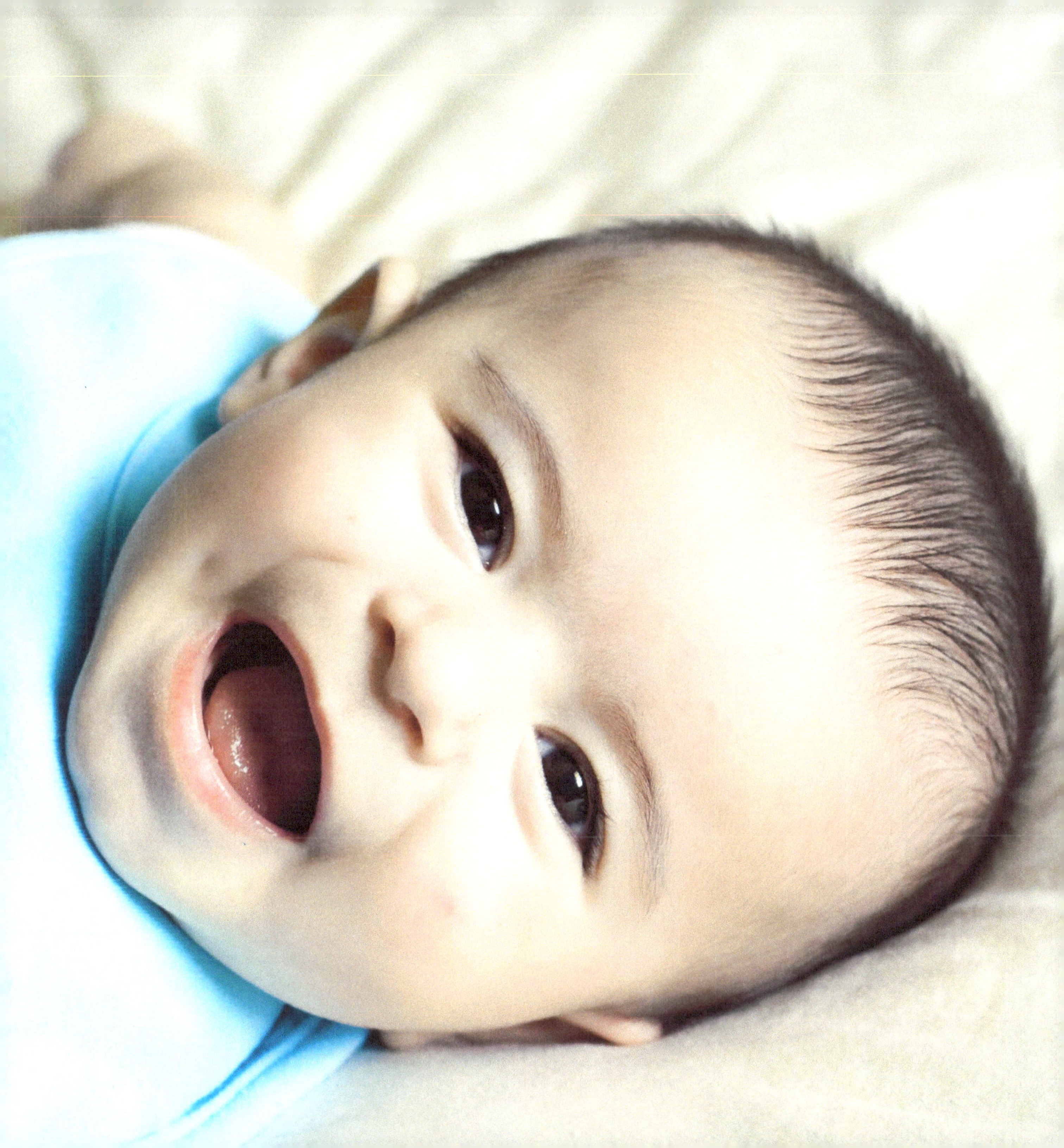

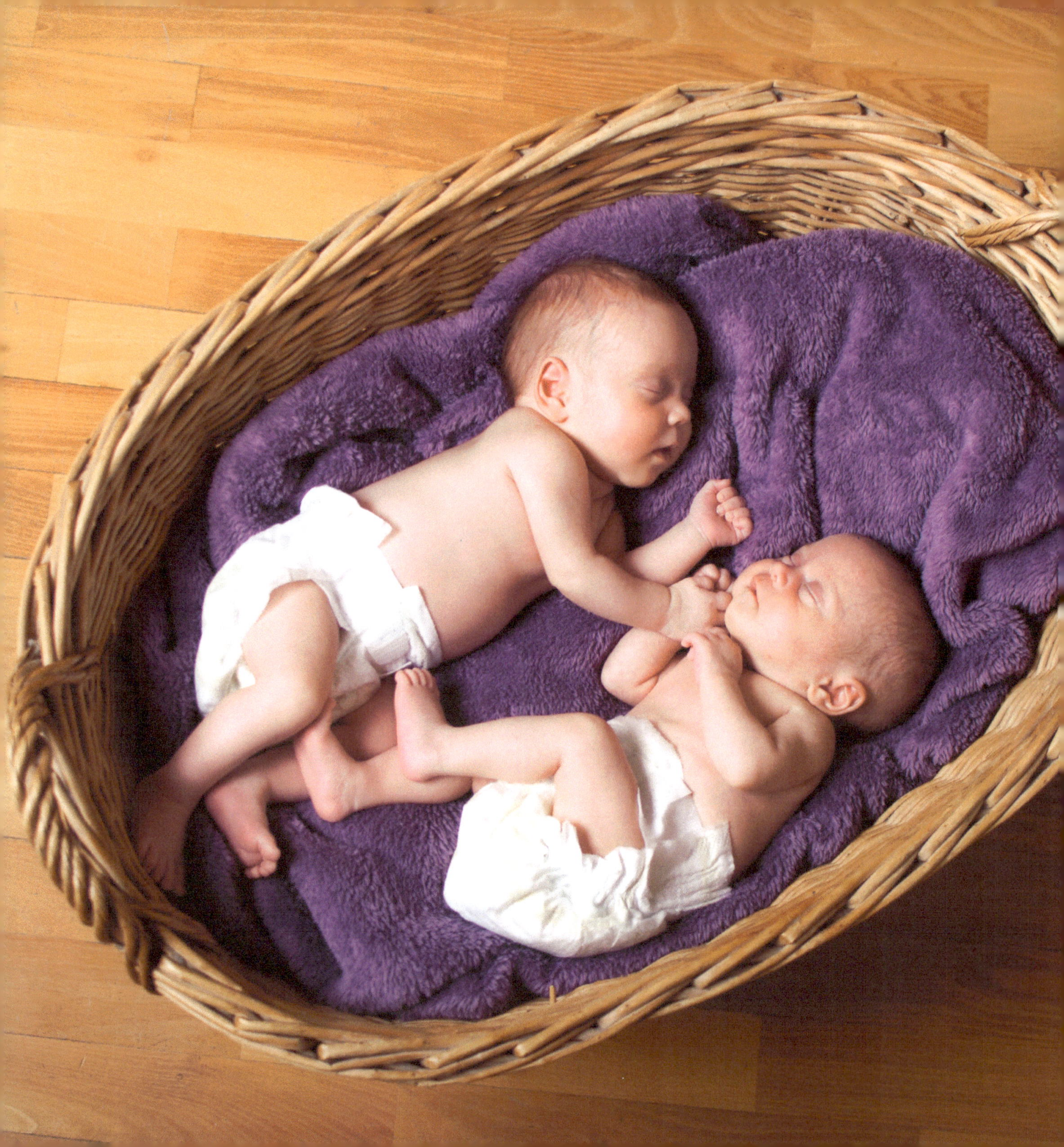

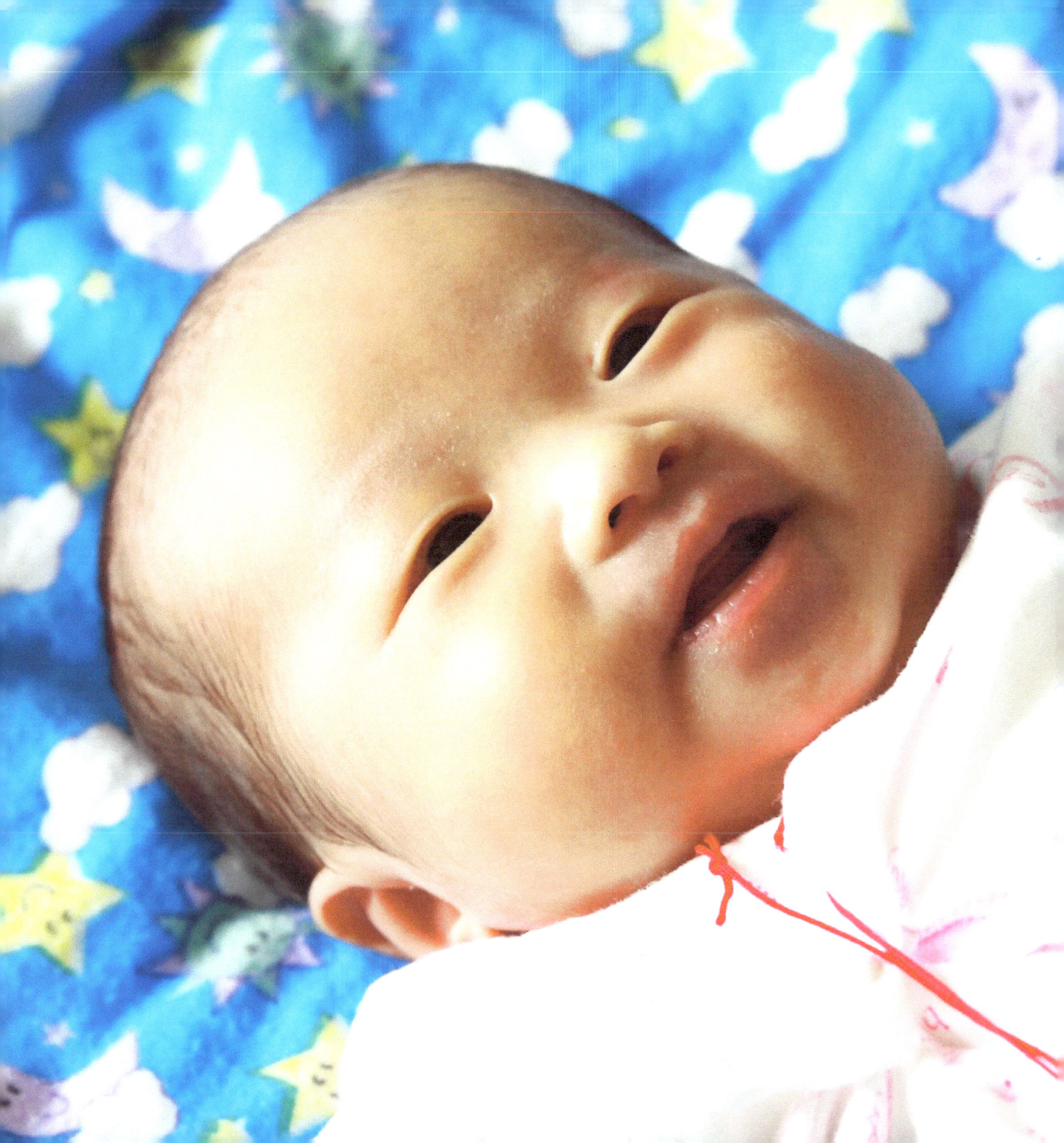

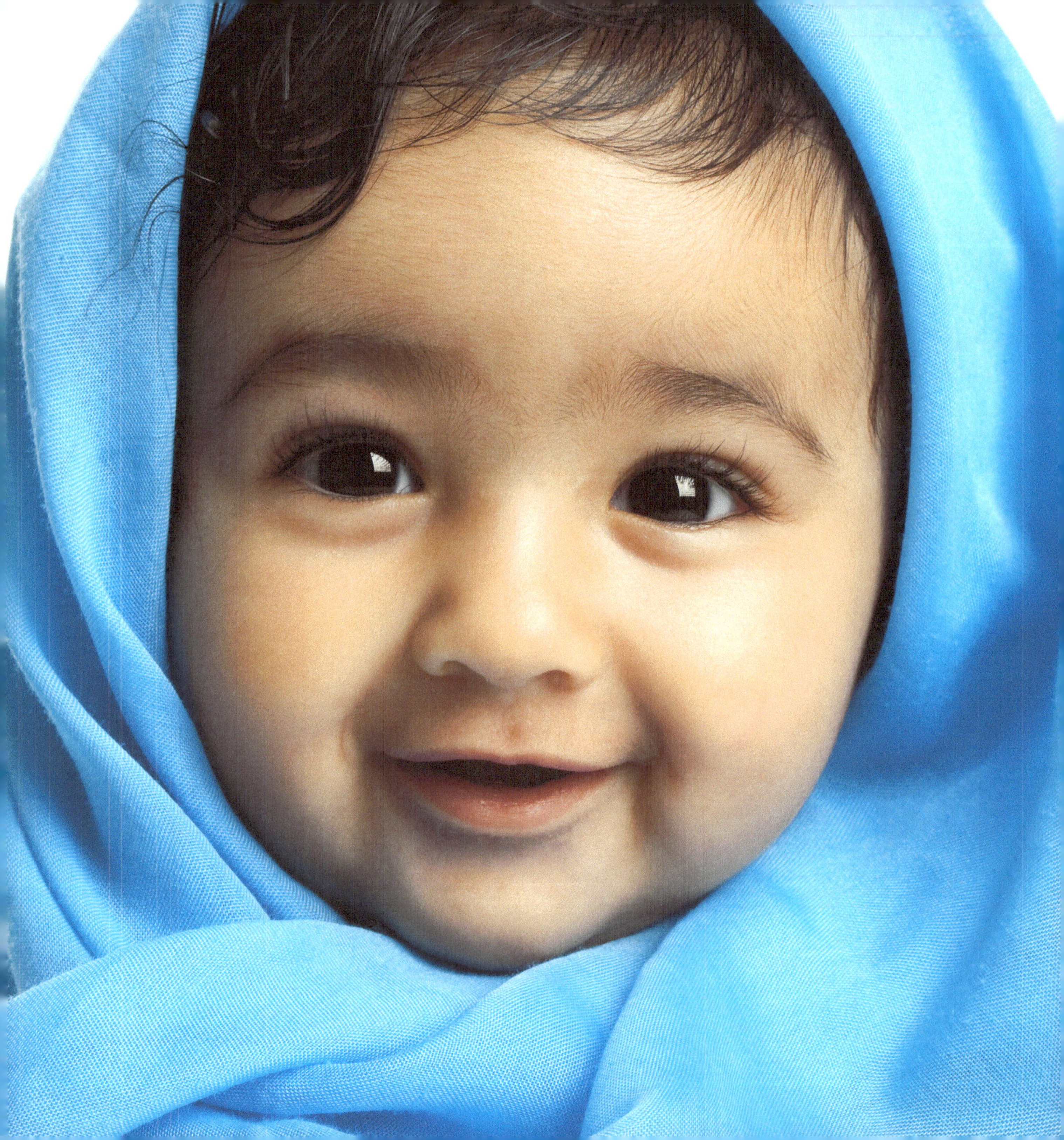

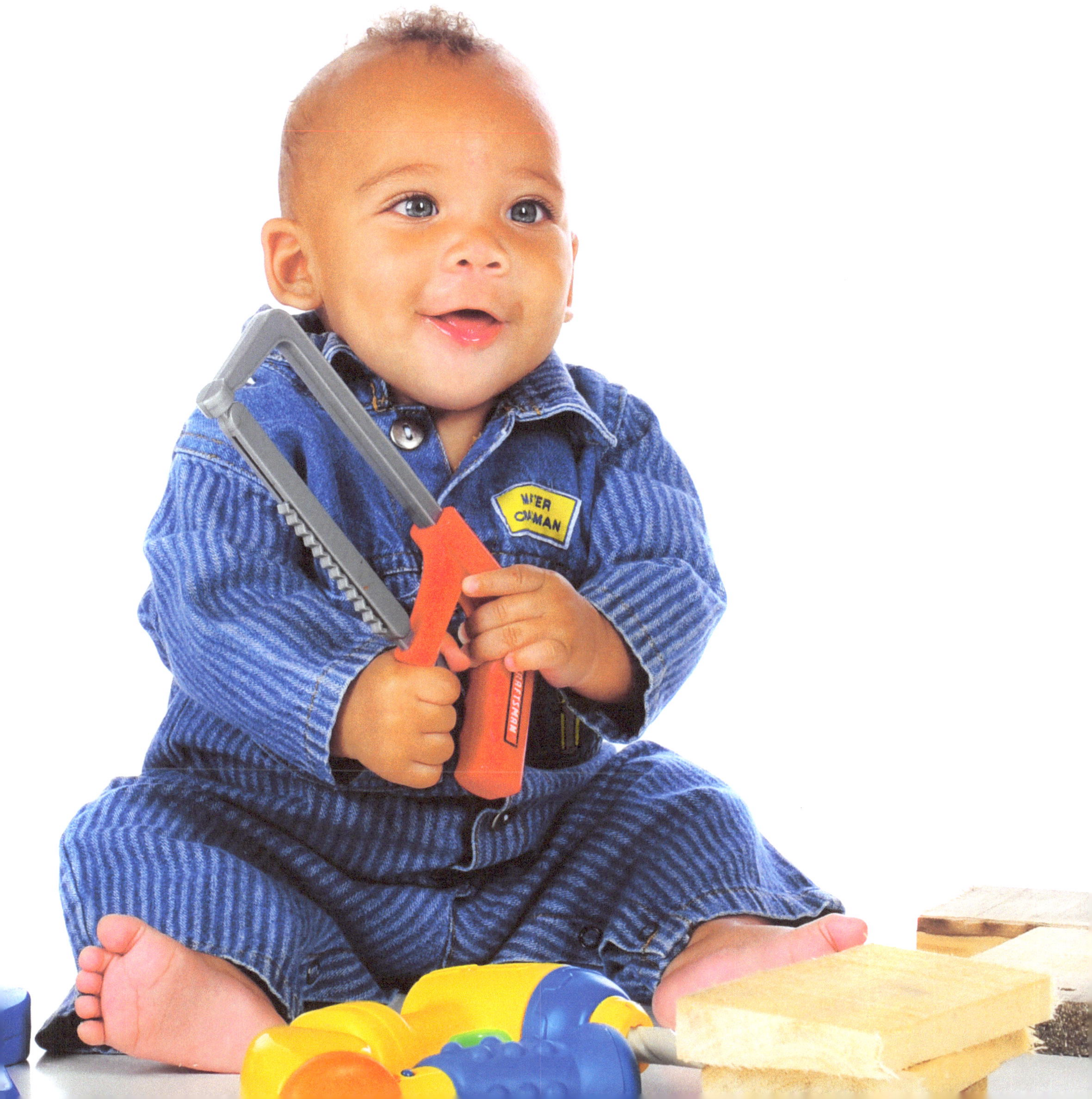

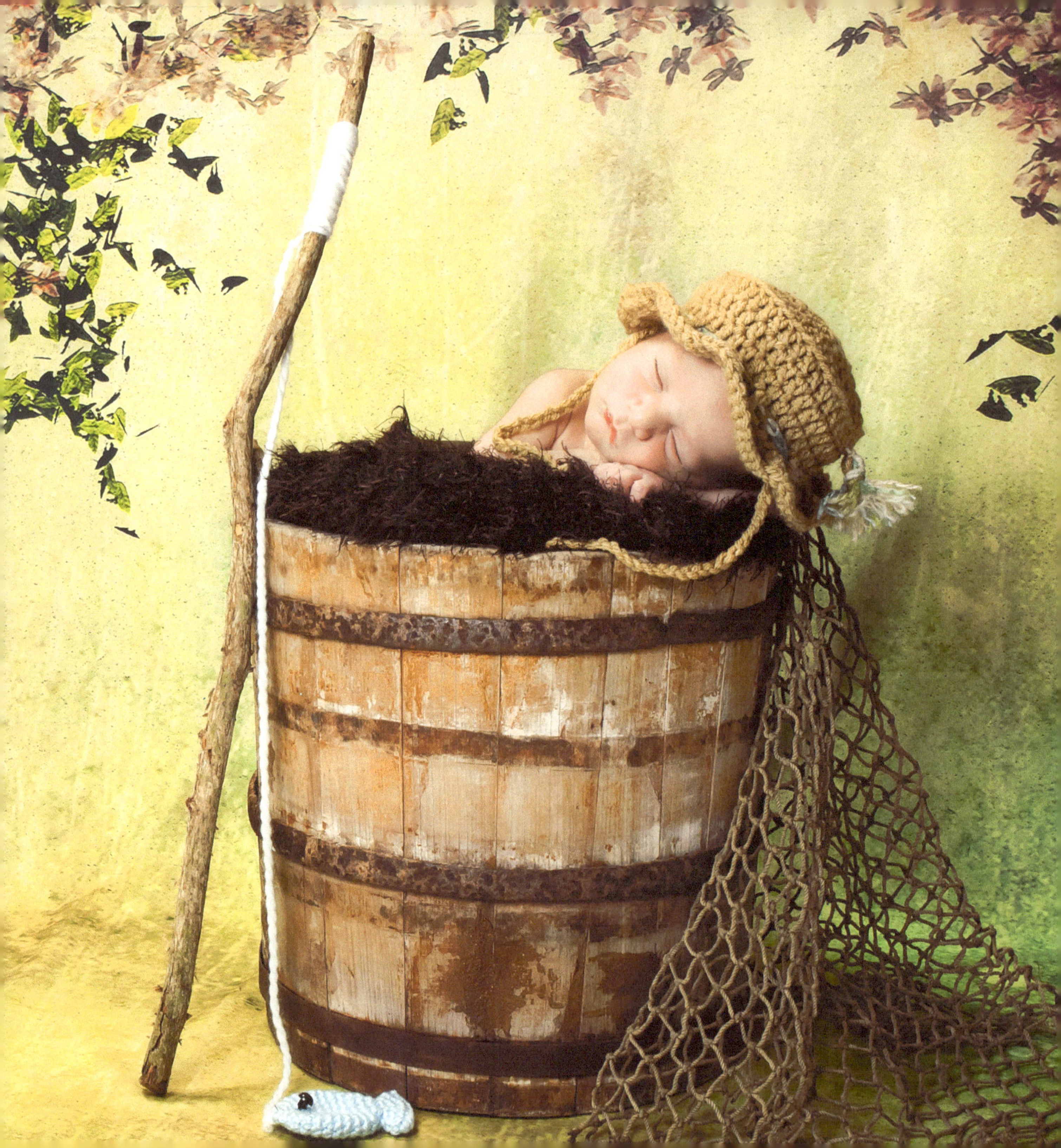

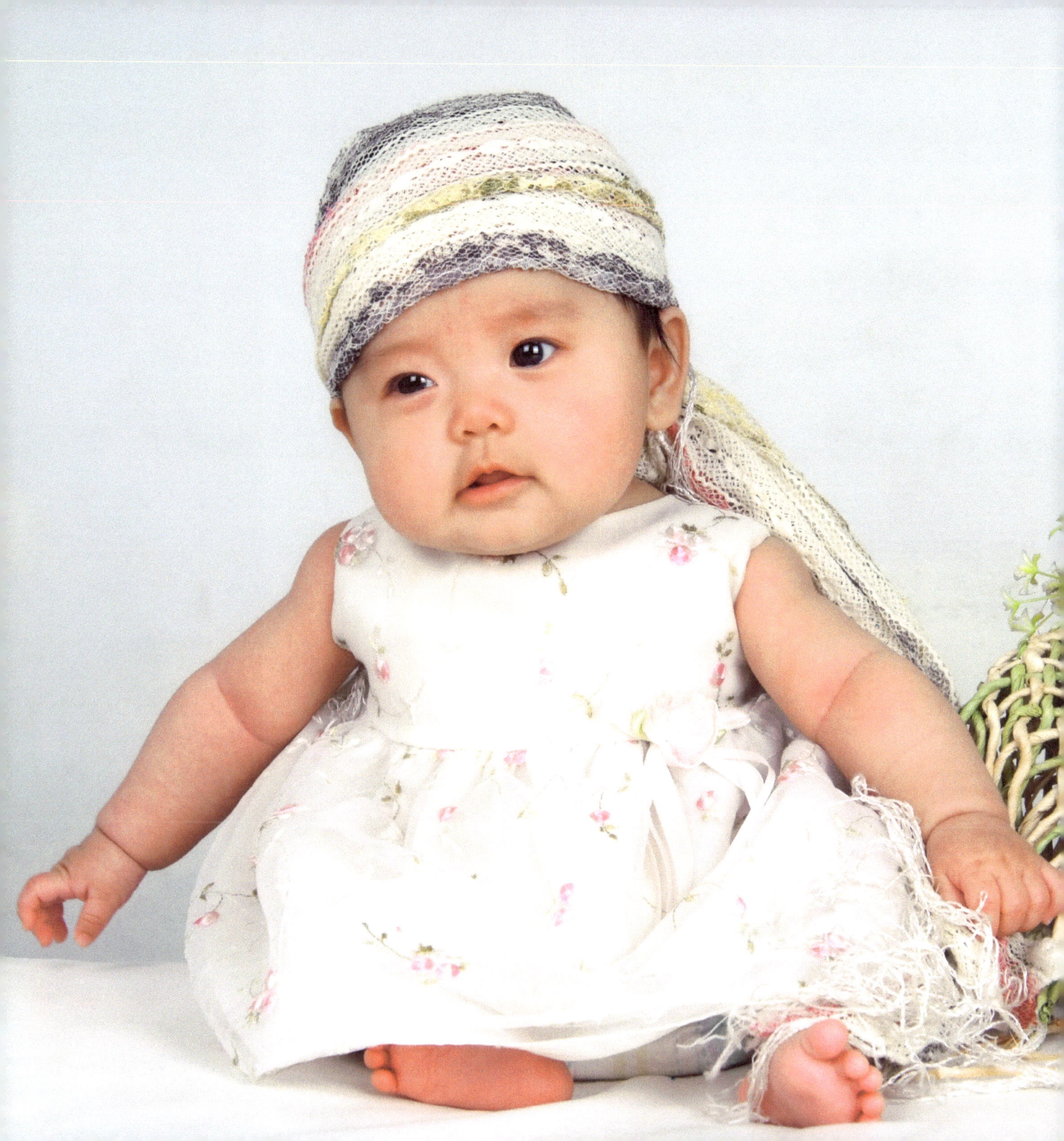

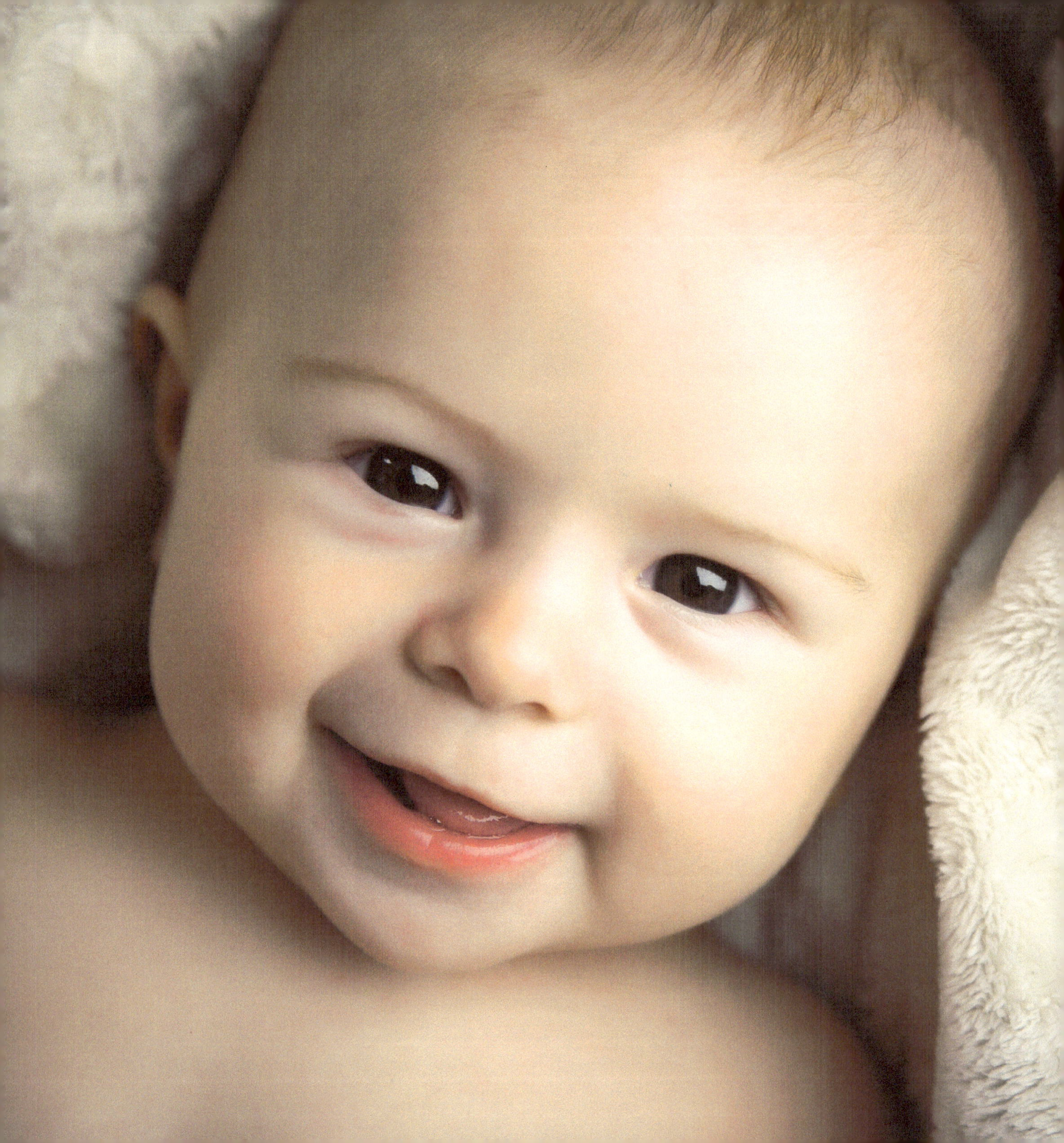

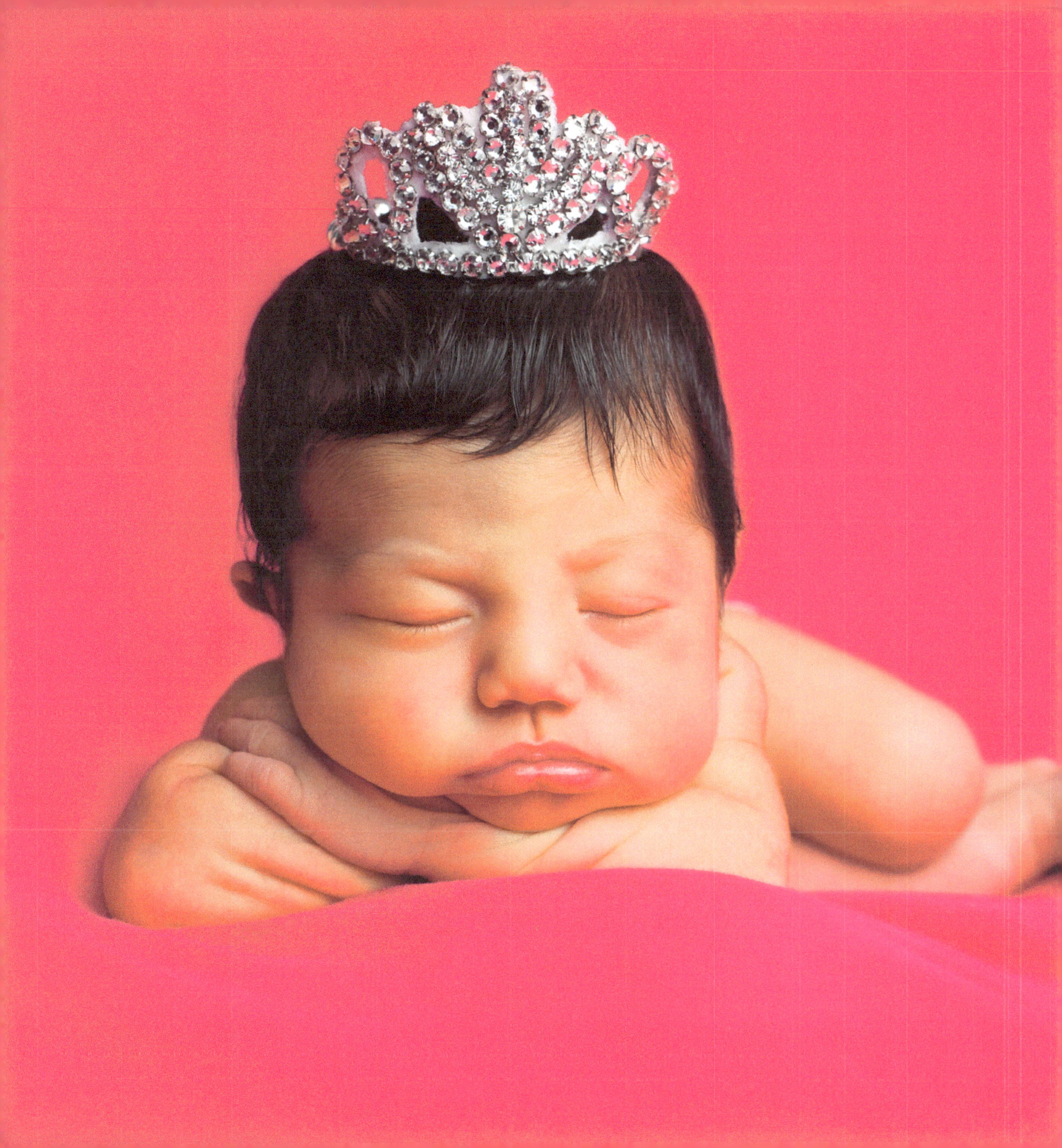

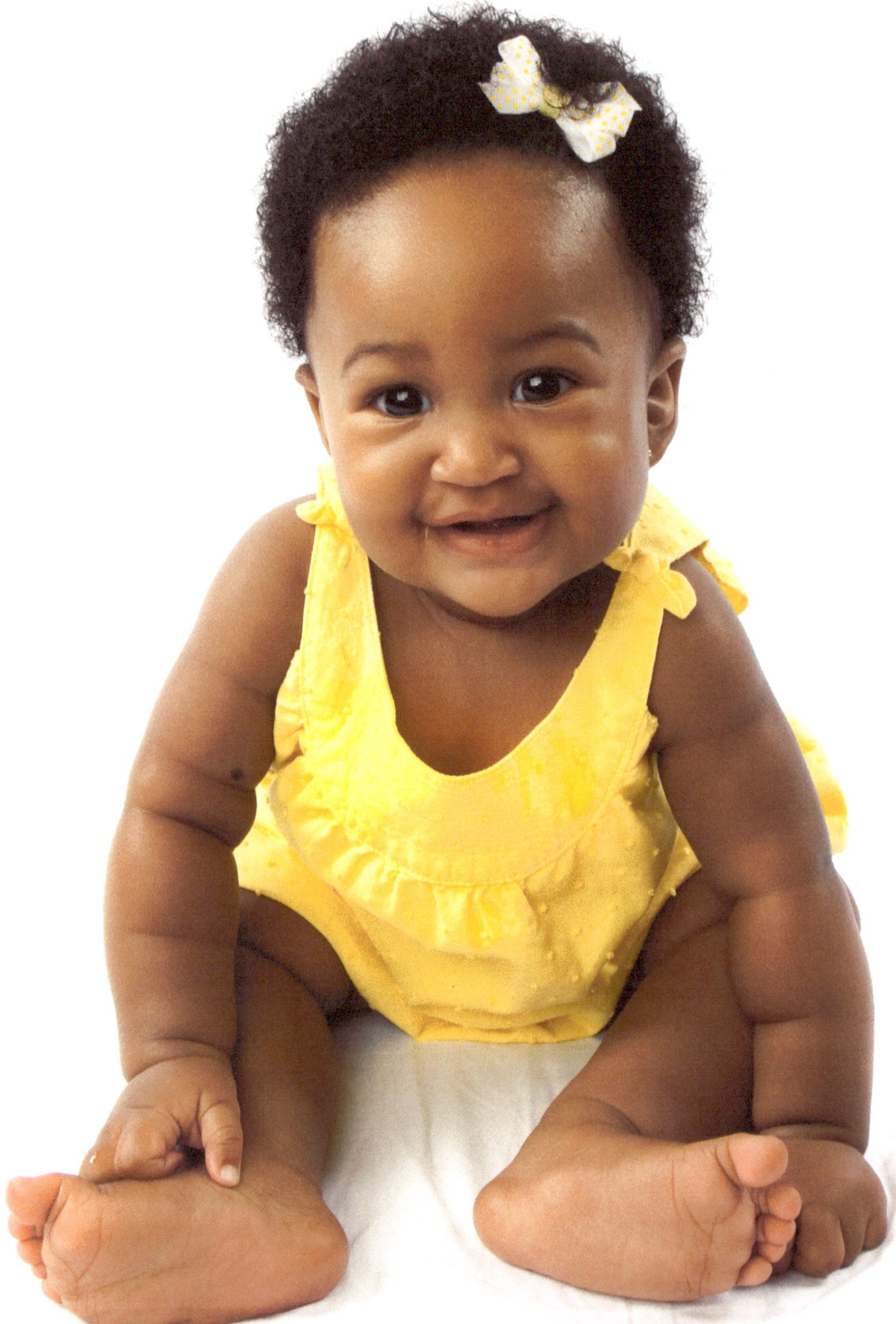

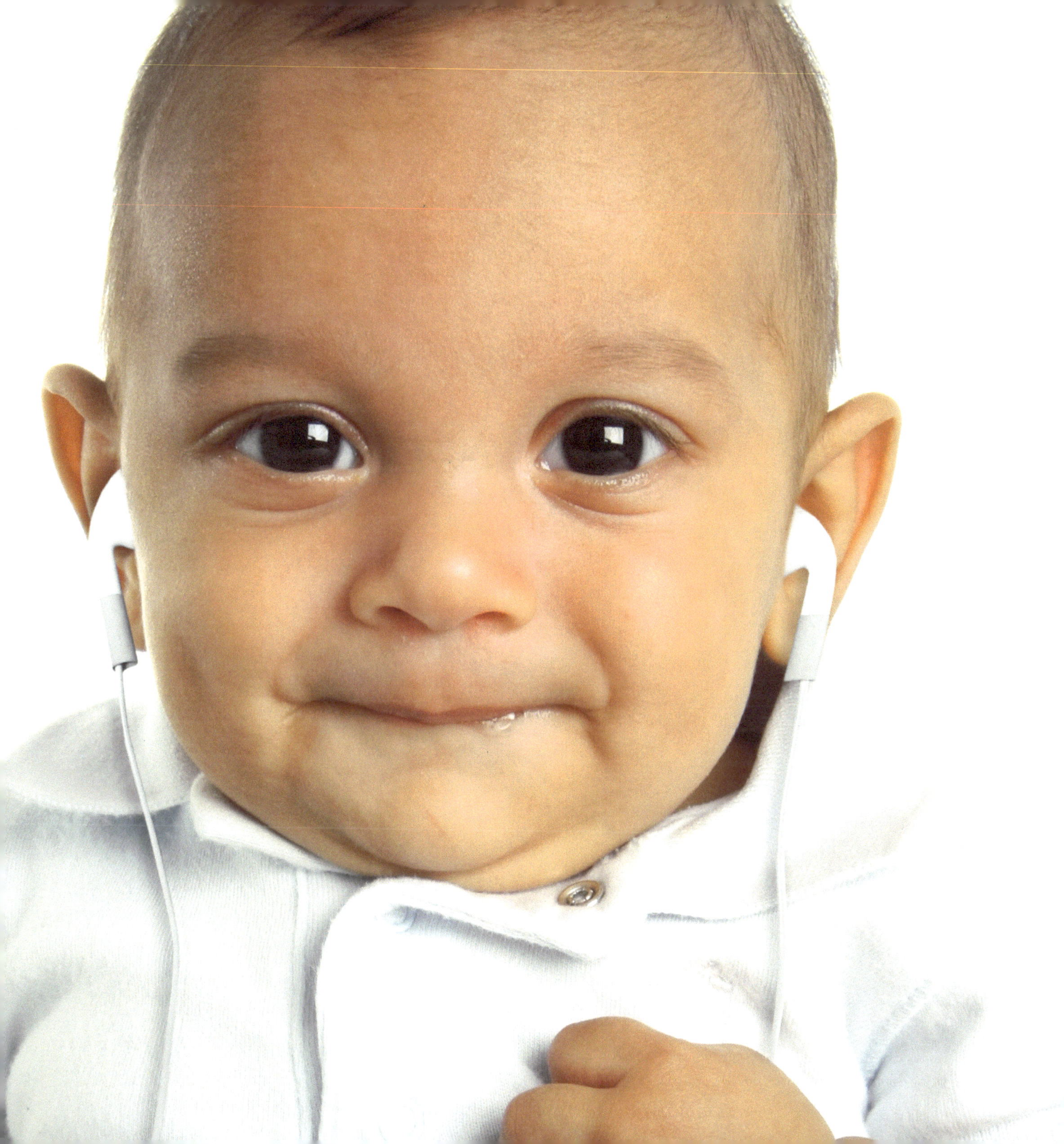

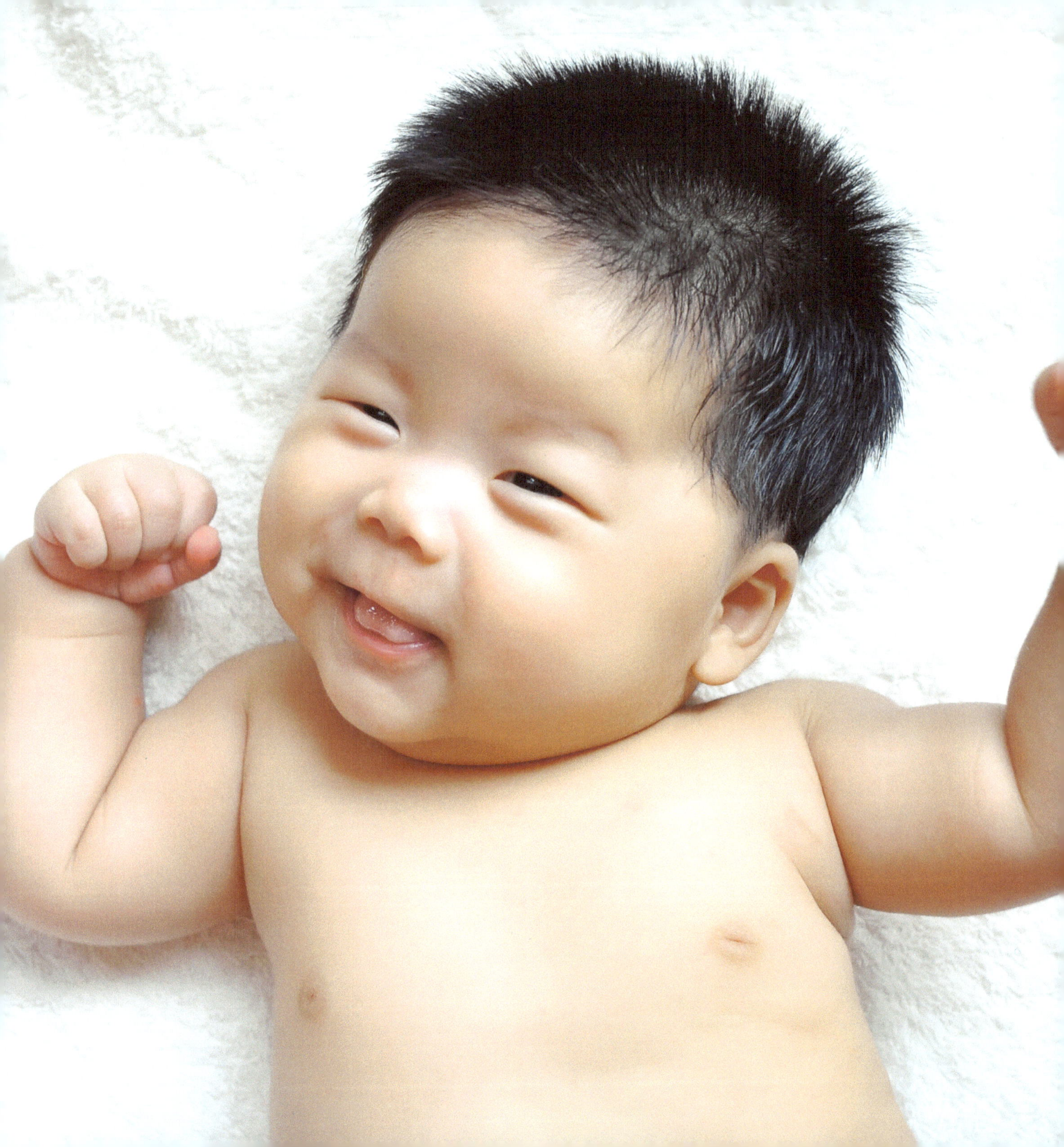

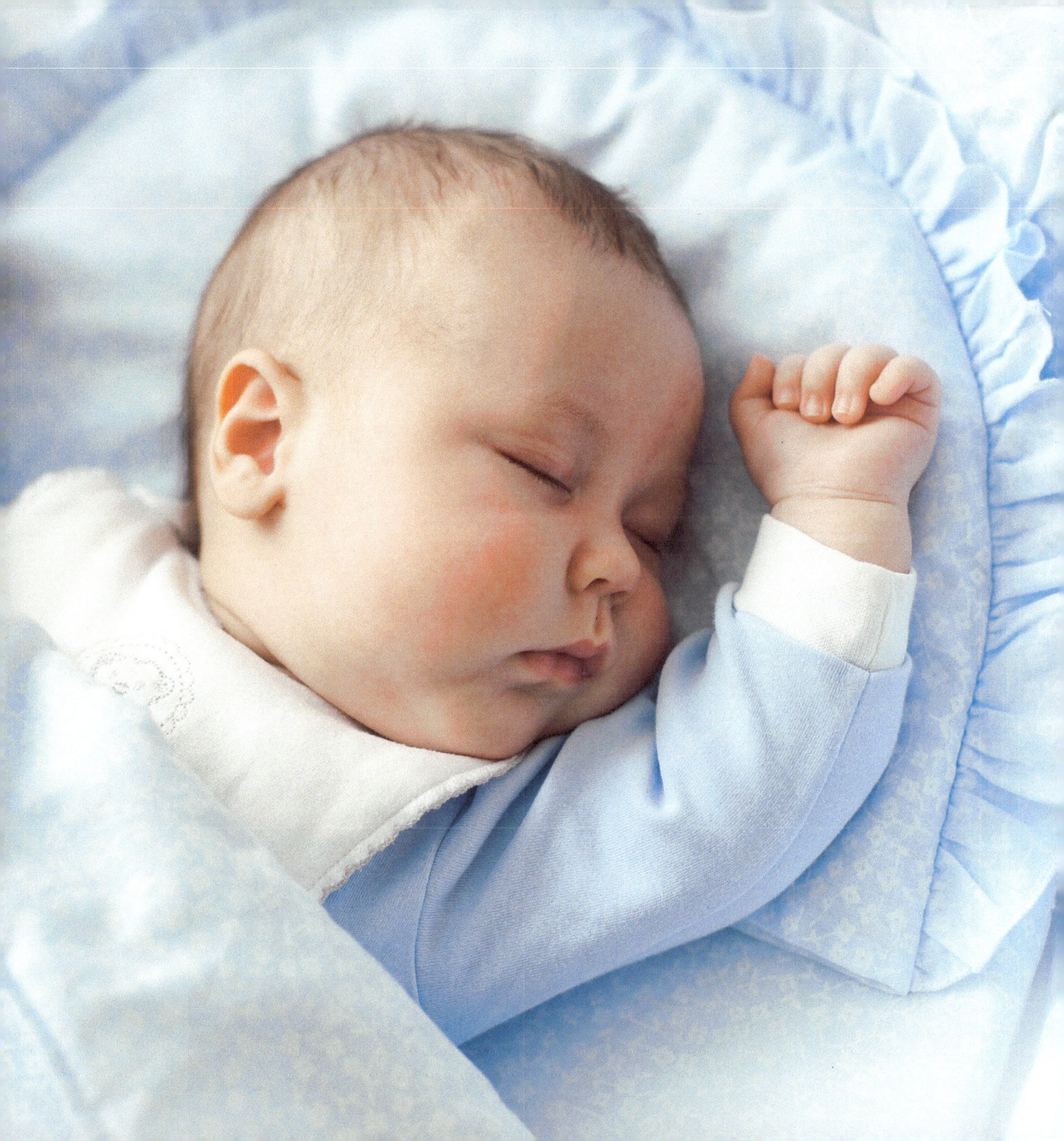

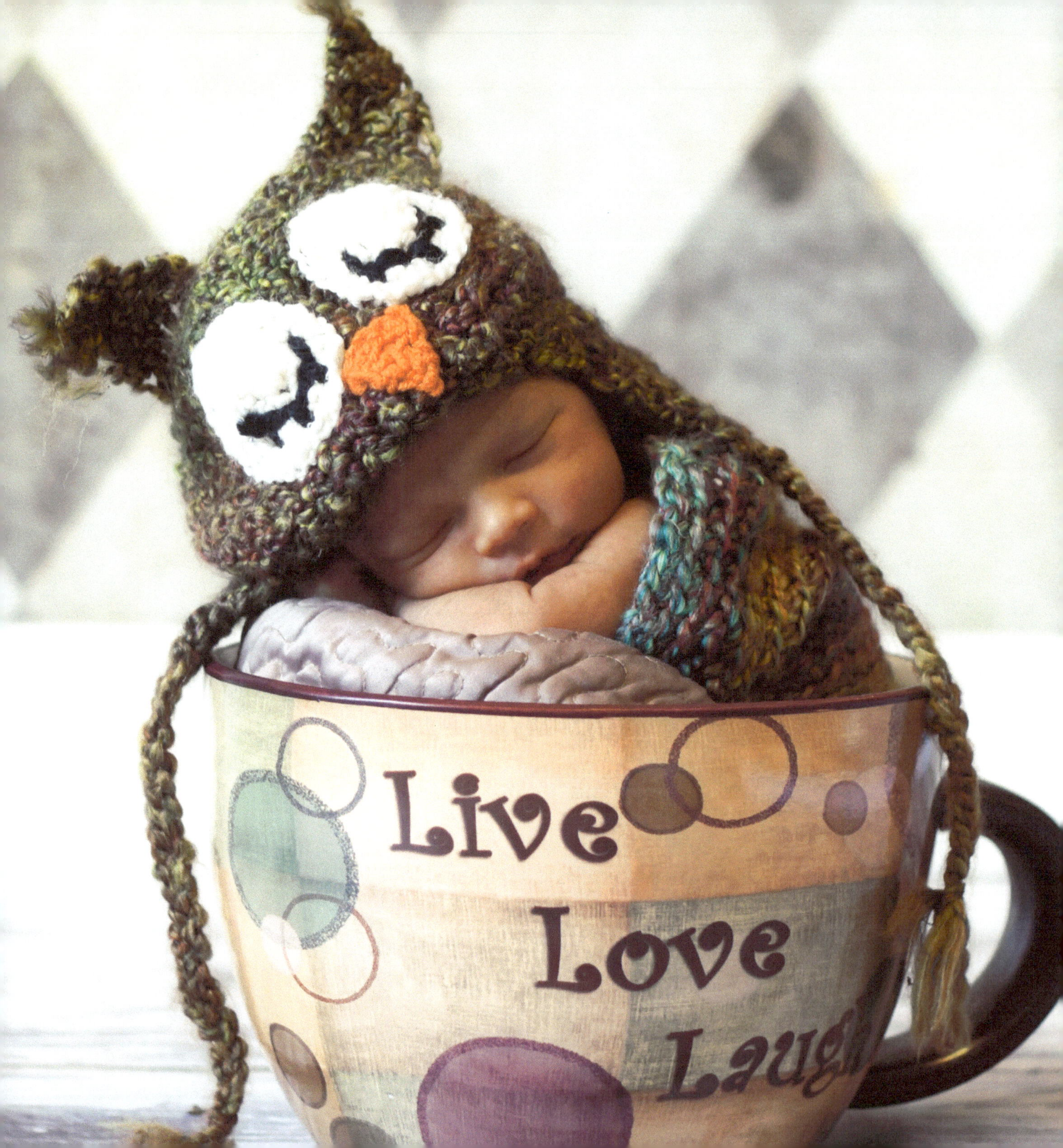
Live
Love

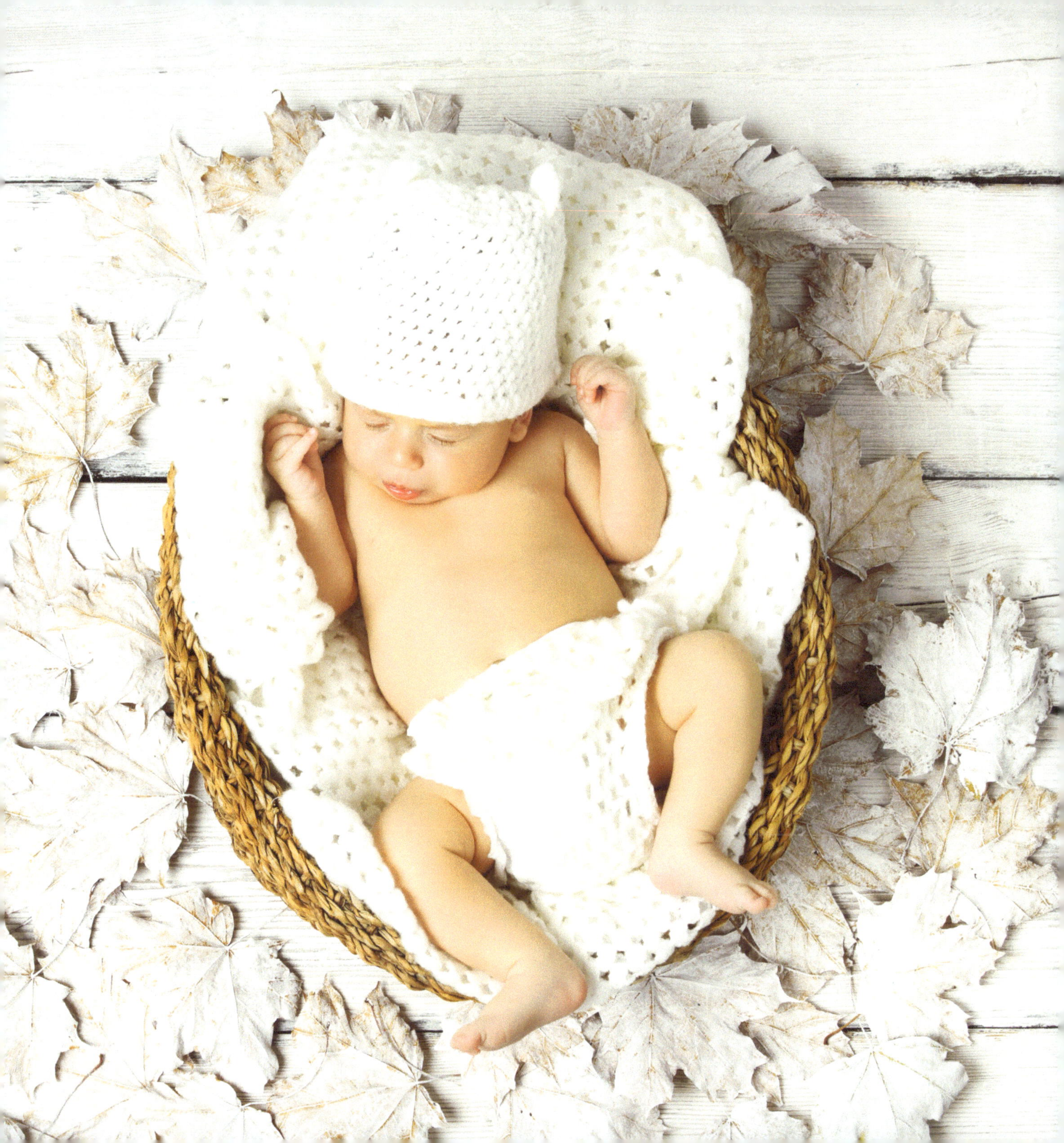

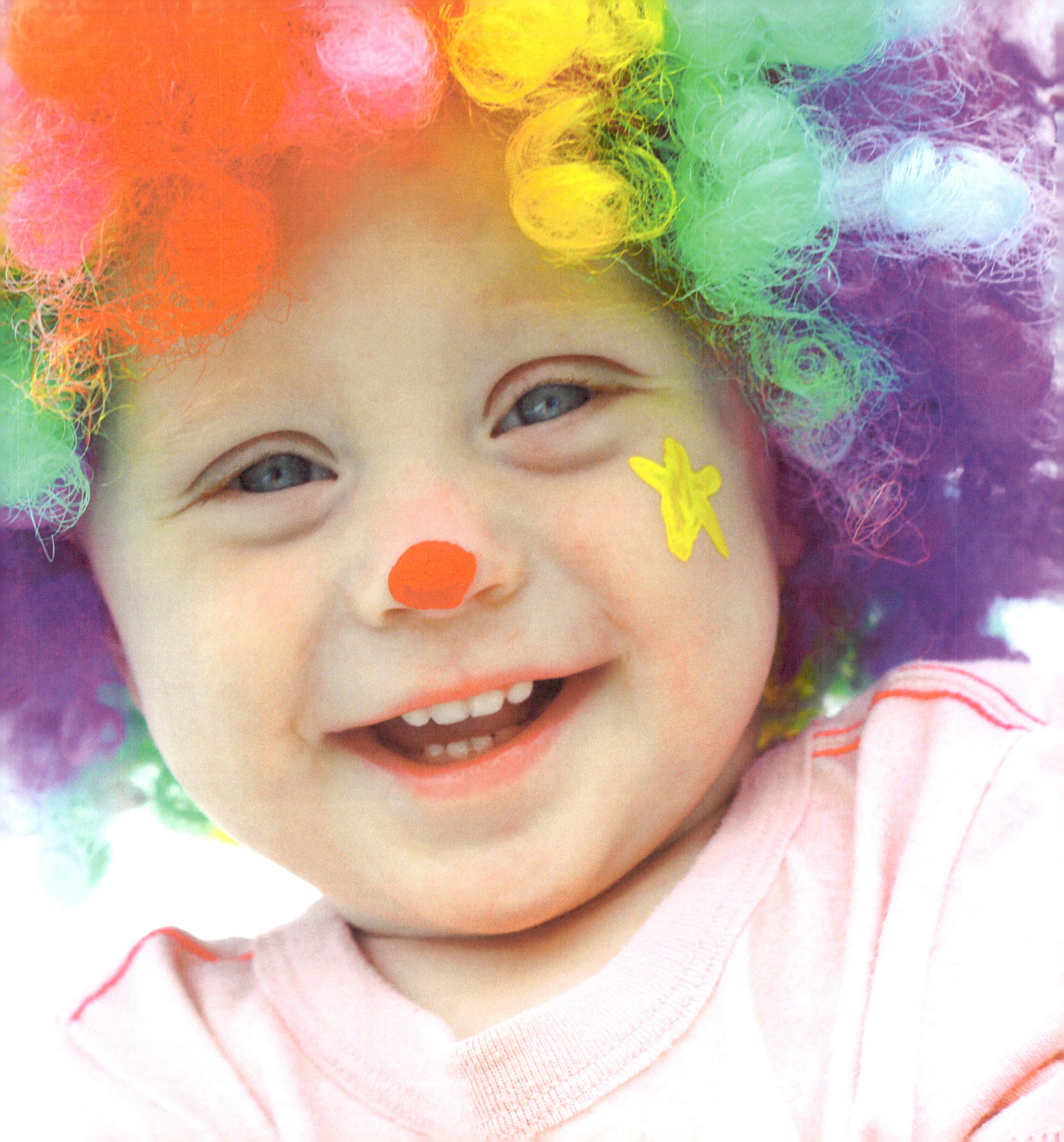

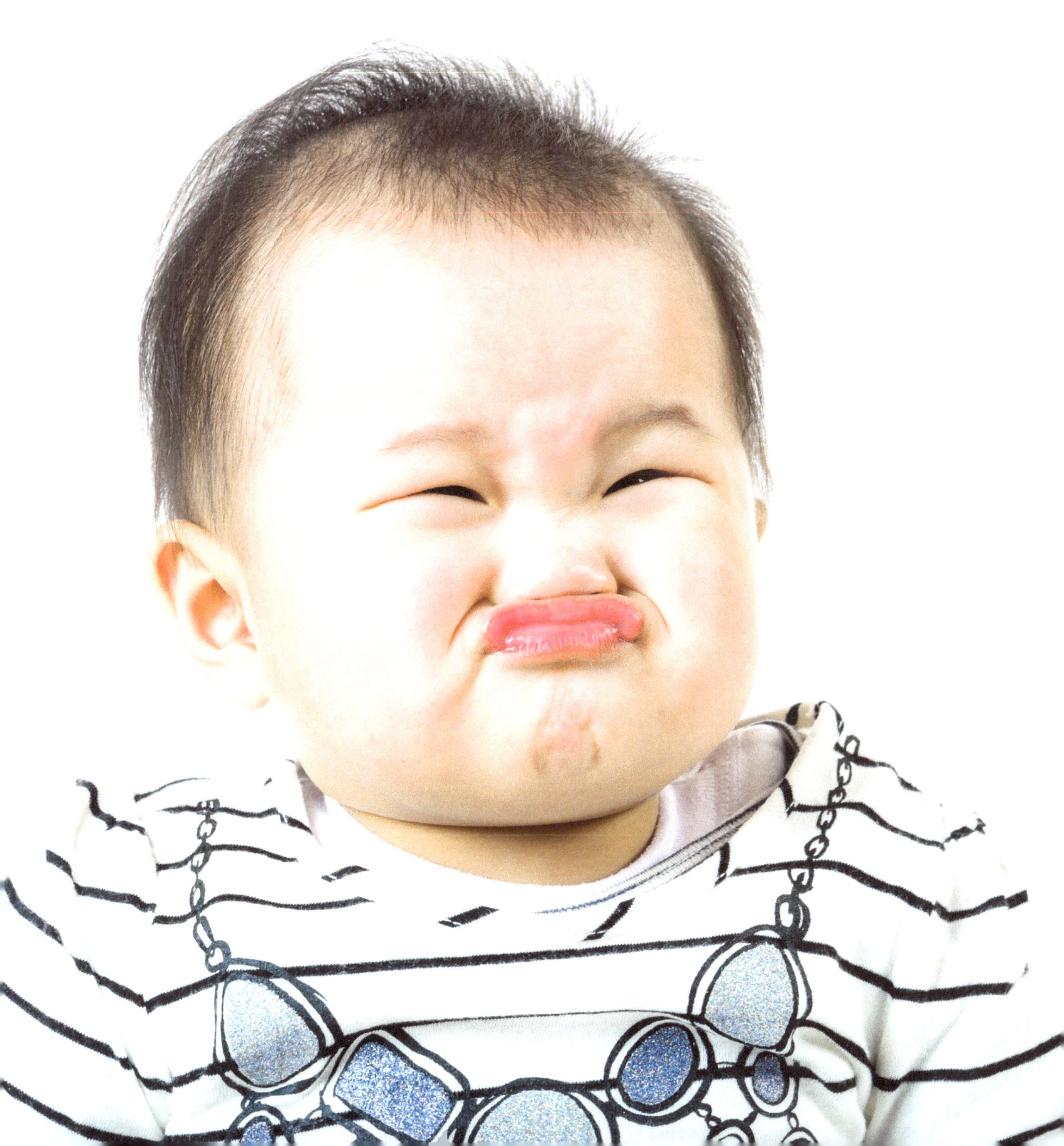

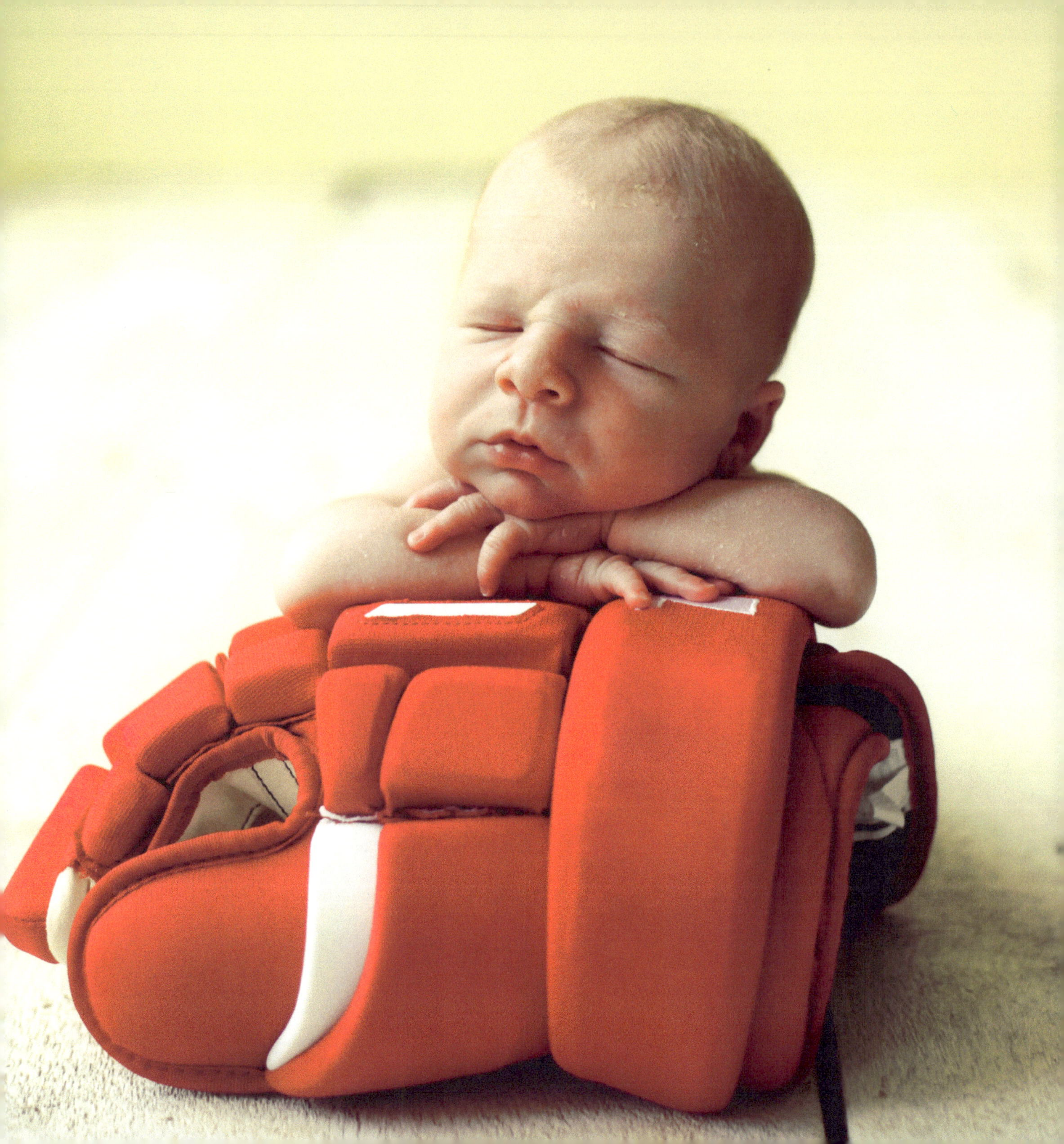

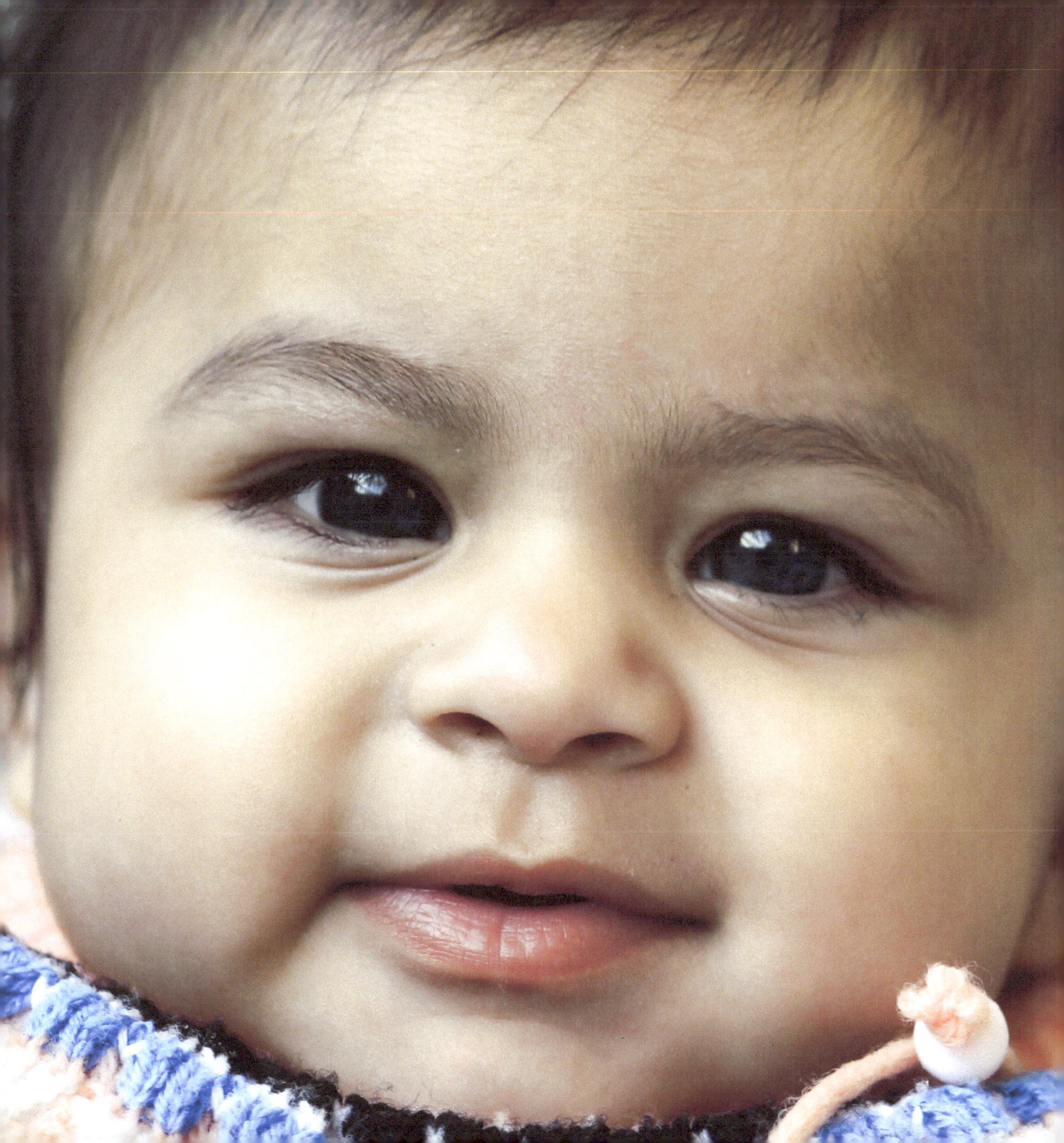

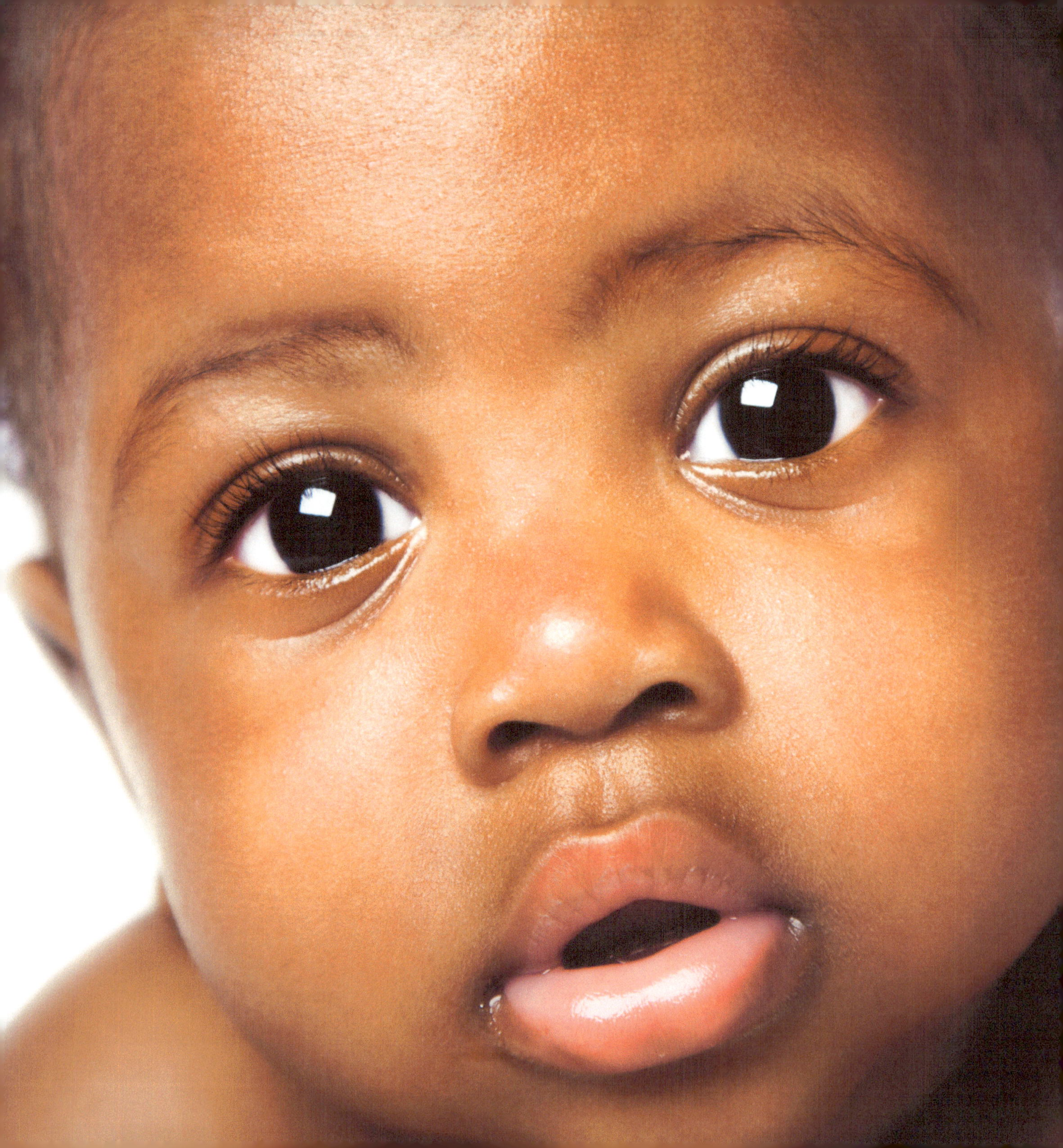

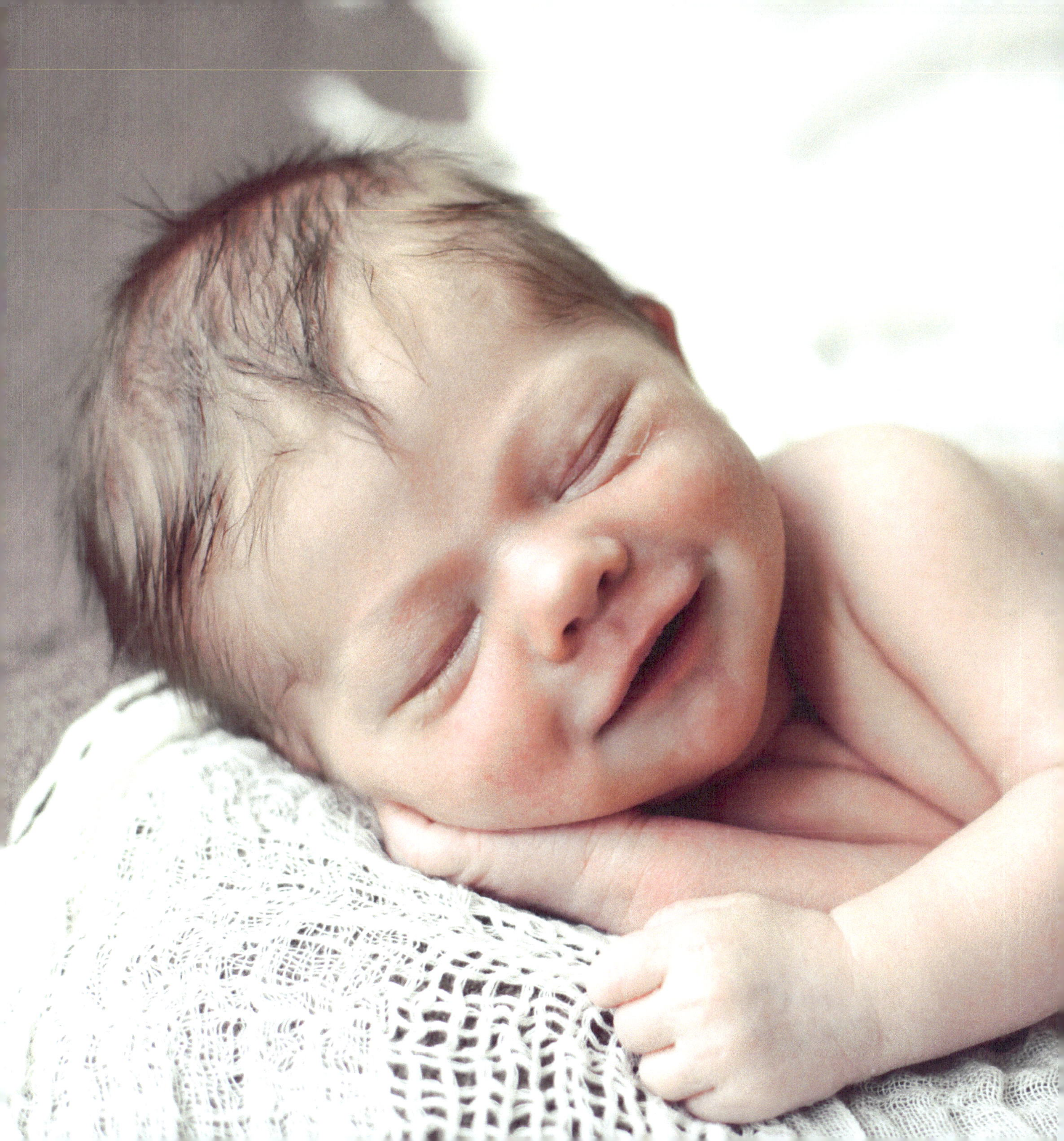

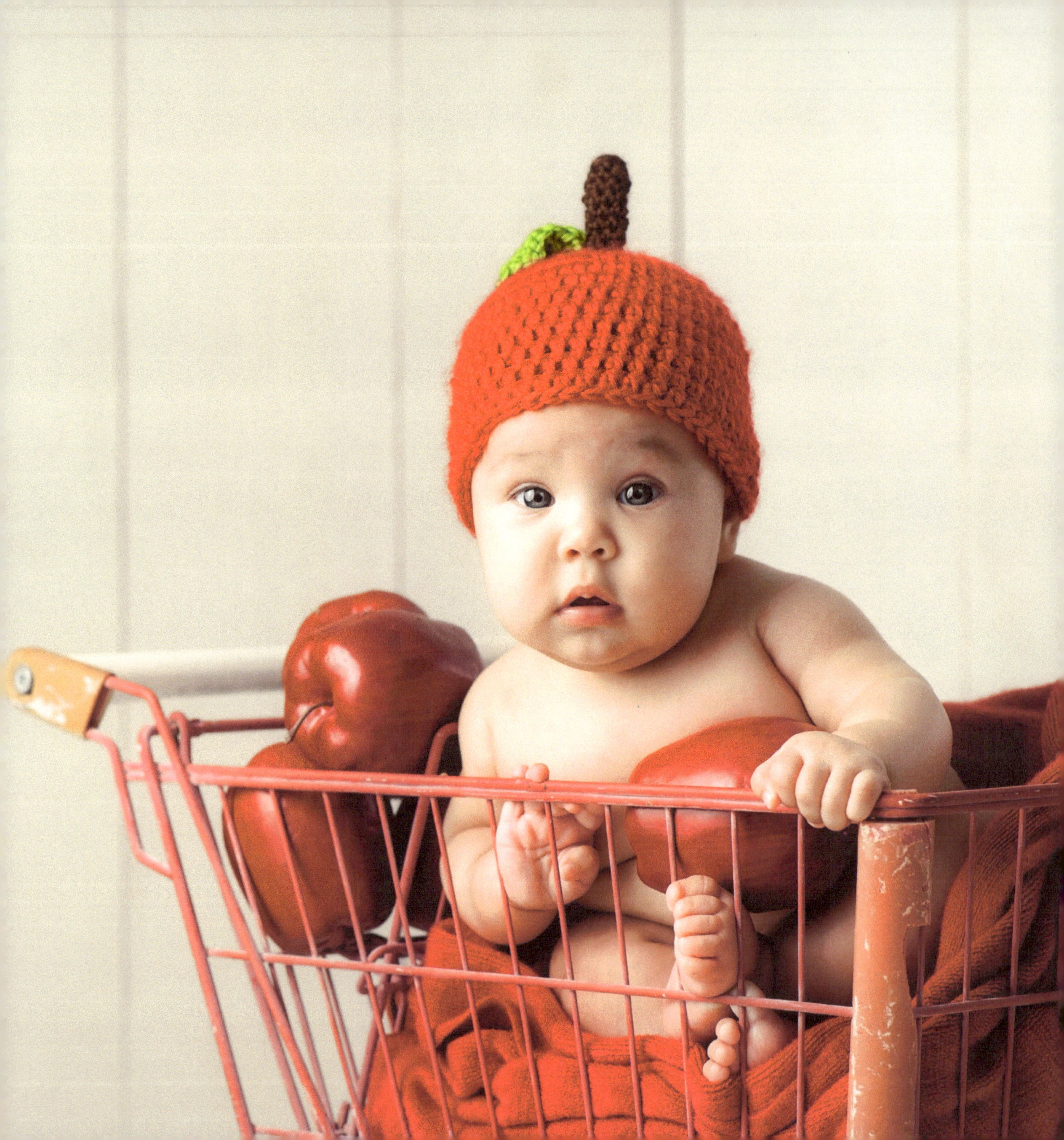

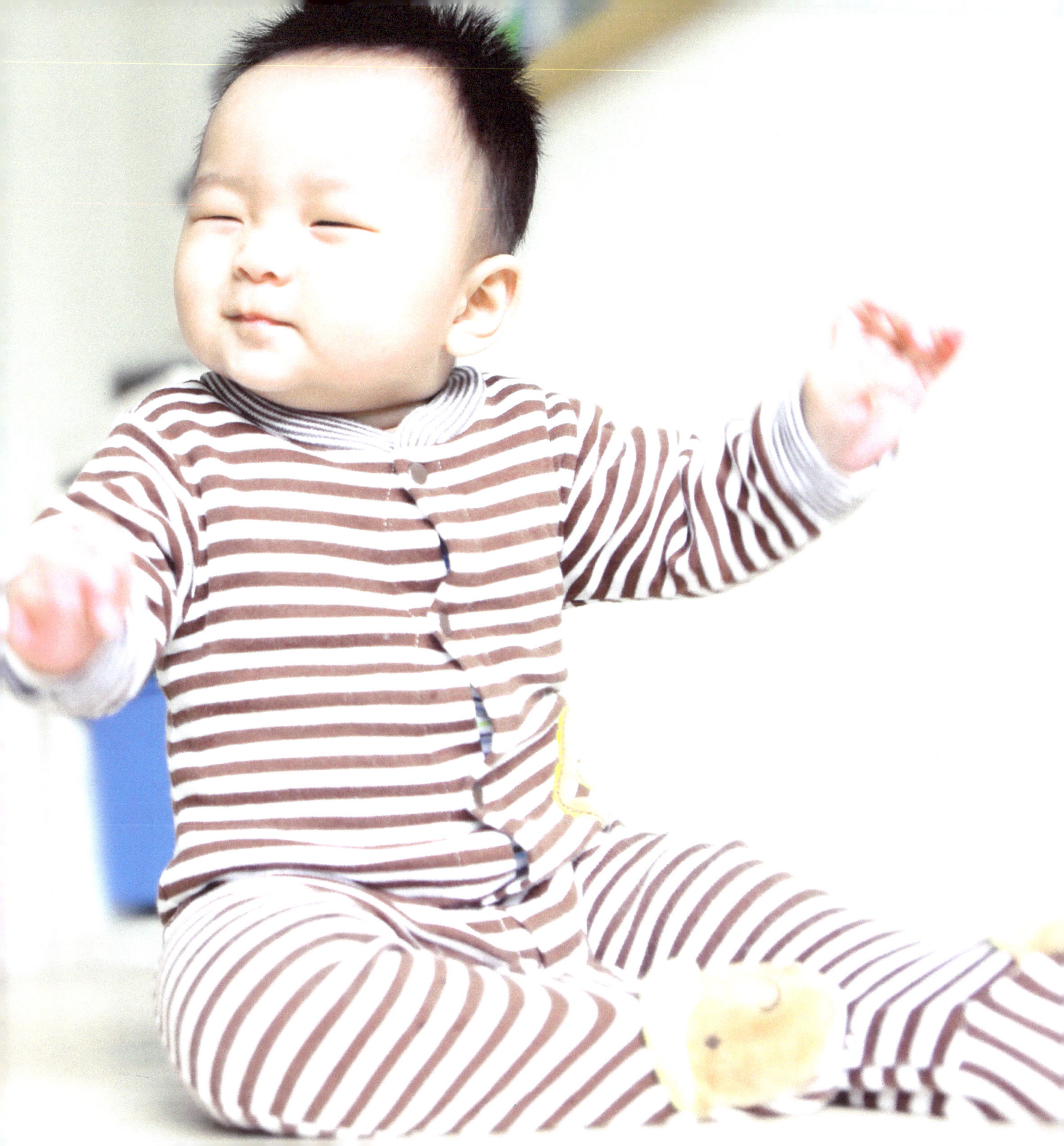

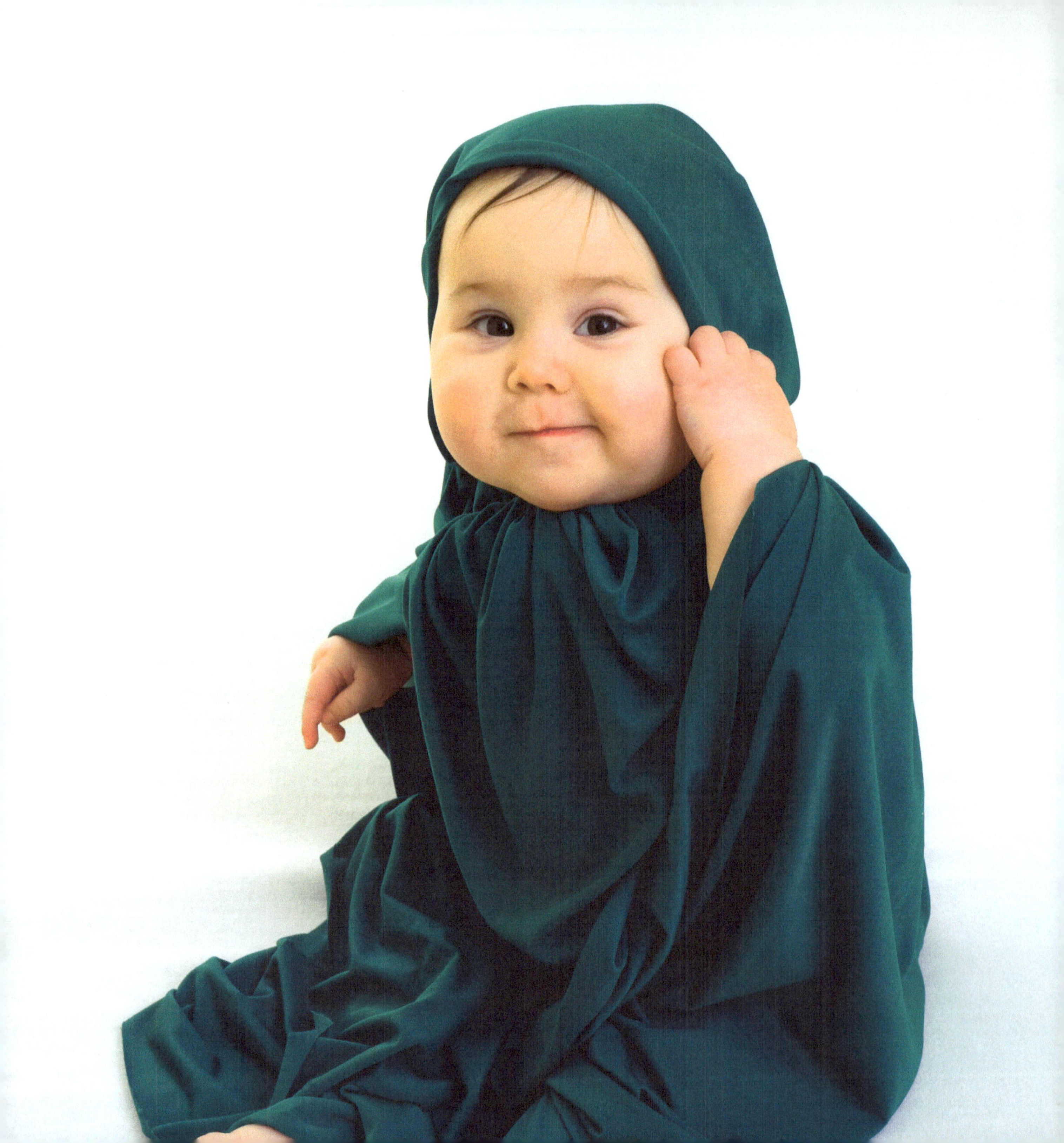

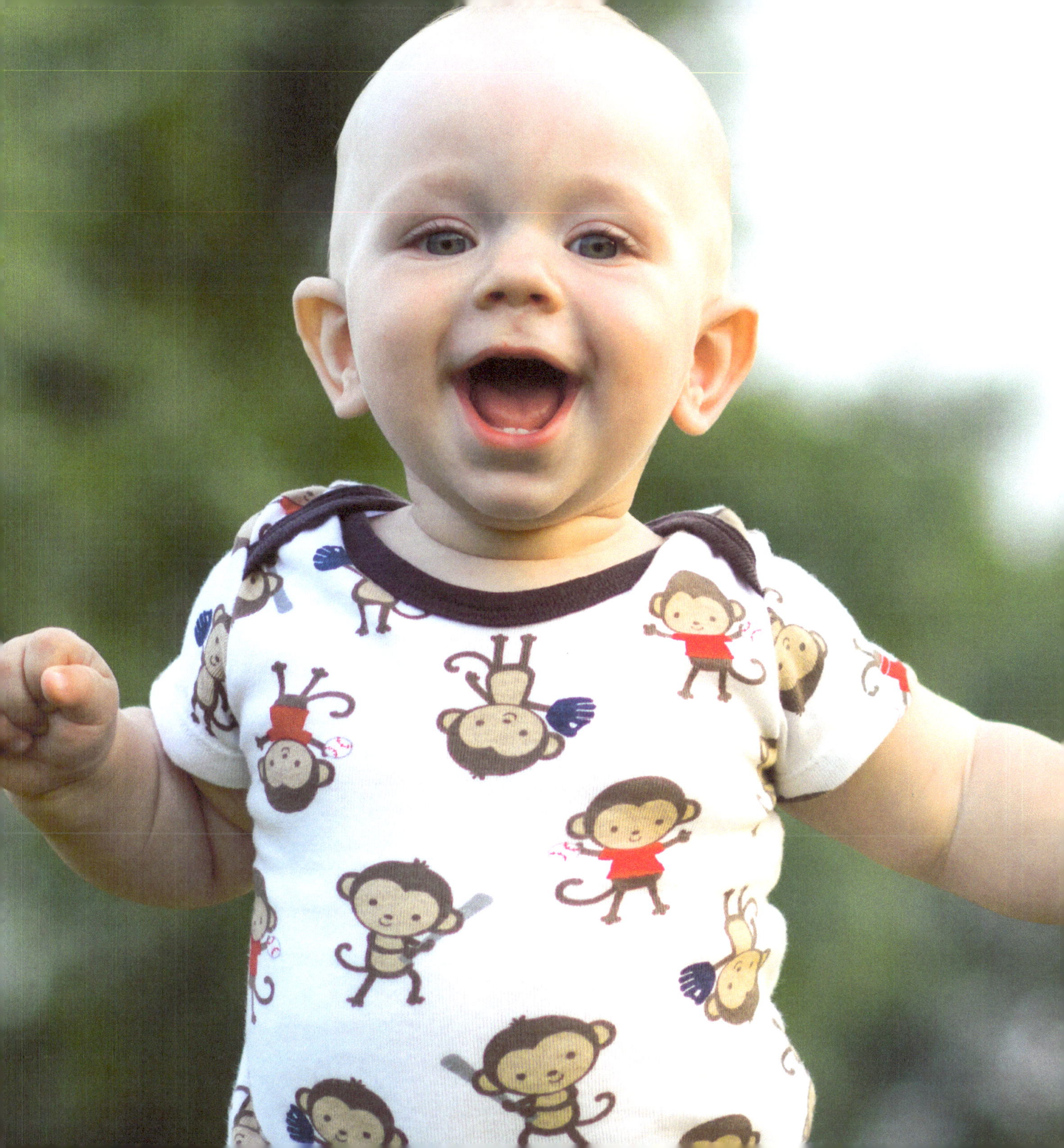

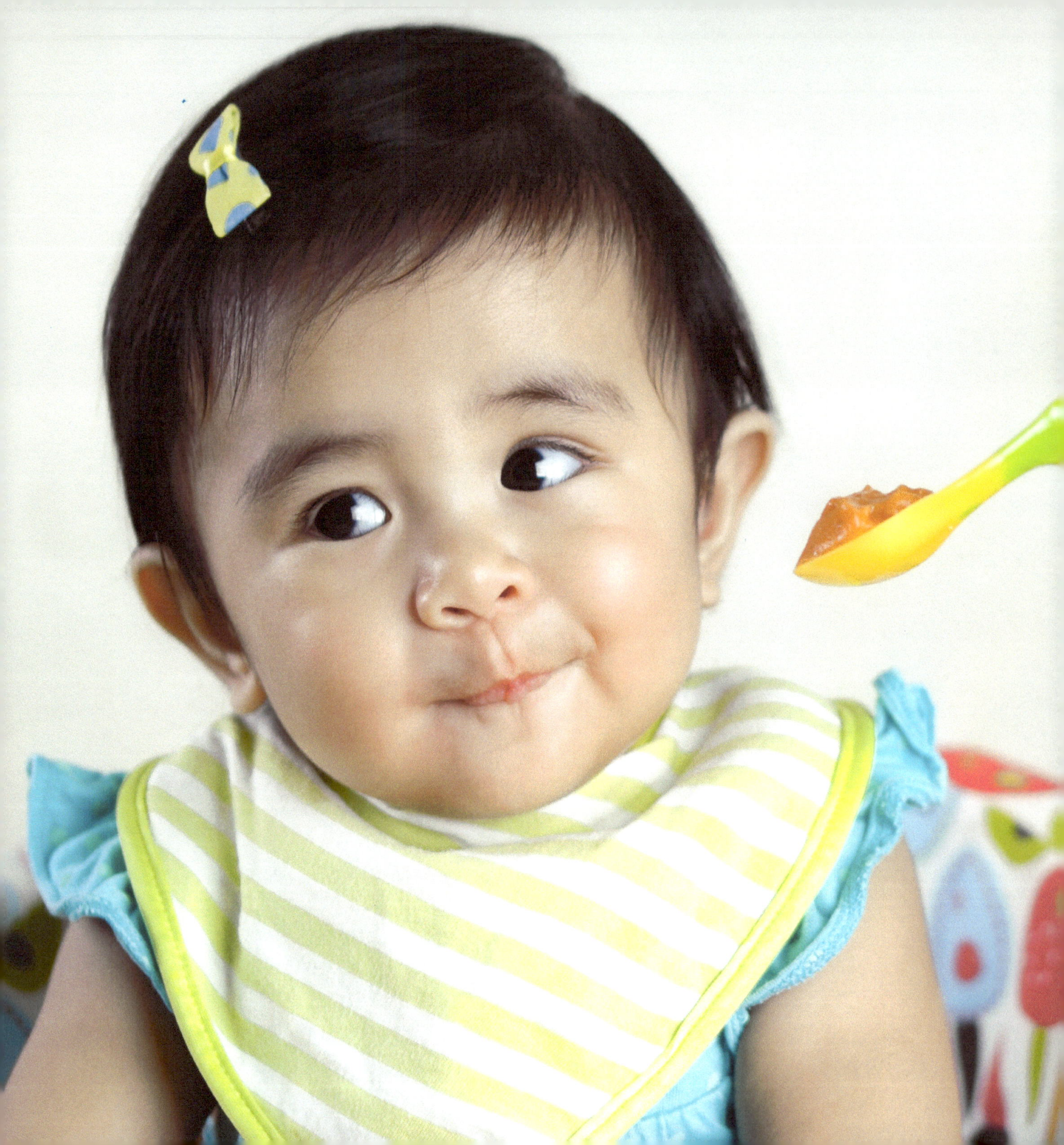

www.ingramcontent.com/pod-product-compliance
Ingram Content Group UK Ltd.
Pitfield, Milton Keynes, MK11 3LW, UK
UKHW061031310726
14089UKWH00009B/191